THE MAN BEHIND BADGE # 711

THOMAS COONEY
WITH MARK YABONSKY

outskirtspress
DENVER, COLORADO

Outskirts Press, Inc.
http://www.outskirtspress.com

ISBN: 978-1-4787-0912-1

Outskirts Press and the "OP" logo are trademarks belonging to Outskirts Press, Inc.

PRINTED IN THE UNITED STATES OF AMERICA

This book is dedicated to my friend Mark Yablonski, who encouraged me to tell my stories and helped me write them. To my wife, Edie, who was by my side through it all and added the personal touch to my stories. To my children and my grandchildren, to better understand why I loved this job. To the firemen who lived through these stories with me. And to all the firefighters who risk their life and all the firefighters who gave their life.

Table of Contents

CHAPTER 1

He may not have realized it as a young boy, but Tom Cooney was destined for a life of public service and, one way or another, helping his fellow man. Born in New York City in January of 1934, he was the youngest of two children and, along with his mother and father, made up their Irish-Catholic family. The lessons and skills he managed to develop growing up, he was able to put to good use by serving a two-year tour as a corporal in the U.S. Army; a twenty-year career with the New York City Fire Department; and chauffeuring for editor, author, and commentator, Mr. W. F. Buckley. Later he became a State Corrections Officer.

Looking back on his youth, Cooney remembered many happy memories from growing up in Queens, New York. Among the many, one in particular that left a lasting impression was the excitement and commotion at the end of World War II, and attending the victory block parties with his family. In celebration of the end of the war and return of the troops, neighborhoods would stage huge block parties. The street would be closed to traffic and people would come from neighboring blocks with covered dishes, refreshments, music, and flags to celebrate. This went on for several weeks, with the party continually moving to different blocks.

Cooney attended St. Joseph's Parochial School in Astoria, Queens, and after graduating from William Cullen Bryant High School, he registered for the draft, which was a mandatory requirement at the time. His love of the sea made him think he would rather be a sailor than a soldier, when his time came to serve his country. With that in mind, he joined the Naval Reserve and spent the next two years attending monthly reserve meetings and going for yearly two-week training sessions at the naval base in Maryland.

In January of 1954, he received his induction notice from the Army and immediately submitted his request to be activated into the Navy. However, due to a major communication mishap and paperwork glitch, his Naval orders never came through on time, and Cooney found himself a private in the Army. Shortly after he completed his Army basic training, he received a letter from the Navy Department informing him he was in violation for failing to report for his Navy basic training. Since he had already finished his eight weeks

CHAPTER 1

of basic training in the Army, and lost fifty pounds in the process, he decided to finish the rest of his tour of duty as a soldier.

By June of 1954, Cooney was on his way to Camp Chaffe, Arkansas, for advanced artillery training. During the last week of the course, he received notice that his entire unit was being assigned to post-war occupational duty in Korea, and would be shipped out within the next two weeks. The news caught him by surprise, making for some hurried panic phone calls.

Seems Cooney and his fiancée, Edie, had plans under way to wed during his next furlough. But they quickly changed those plans and decided to marry before he left for Korea. Leaving some very bewildered and uncertain parents behind, Edie flew out to Camp Chaffe, Arkansas, took care of the necessary paperwork, and three days later on July 4, 1954, they were married. To help the couple celebrate the event, the training sergeant surprised them with a three-day pass as a wedding present. When Cooney returned to base three days later, he was made aware that the assignment sheet had been revised again. This time only half of the unit would go to Korea and the other half would be sent to Fort Bragg, North Carolina. Tom recalls he made a dash to the announcement board to check out the new assignment sheet and let out a shout when he found his name on the Fort Bragg list.

Cooney said he had no difficulty settling into his new life at Ft. Bragg, but adapting to life in the south was another matter. This was 1954 and segregation was a way of life in the southern town of Fayetteville, North Carolina. Coming from New York City had not prepared the young couple for blacks and whites having separate restaurants, movie entrances, seating on a bus, etc. At camp there was no such problem, but once they left the base, it was a whole other story.

Tom vividly remembers the time his wife returned from her first shopping trip into town, visibly shaken. Edie had made the mistake of helping an elderly black woman onto the steps of a bus and allowing her to enter the bus before she did. They were both loudly scolded by the white bus driver, in front of the passengers, and told they would both have to exit the bus. Edie argued she was new in town, had just moved to the Army base and was not aware of all the rules in town and to please not blame the elderly woman. Tom believes the mention of the Army base had something to do with the bus driver's decision to allow them to remain on board, since the camp personnel provided a large revenue for the small town.

Another incident, which still bothers Cooney, happened in December of the same year. He and Edie had planned to drive home to Queens for the Christmas weekend and offered two buddies from his barracks, who also lived in Queens, to ride along. On the way north they encountered heavy rain and icy roads and ended up sliding off the road into a small ravine. A truck driver, seeing three soldiers trying to push the car to safety, was kind enough to stop and help. When he left they thanked him and he smiled and said, "Be glad it was me that stopped and not the local police." They continued on their trip, talking about the strange comment the truck driver made. A few miles later they spotted a small diner and decided to stop for coffee. Cooney recalls they all got out of the car and entered the diner, when the man behind the counter suddenly shouted, "Stop right there, we don't serve n---ers in here." They were stunned and started to protest, but their black soldier friend said he did not want any trouble and headed back to the car. They ordered four cups of coffee, but when the owner refused and would only fill three cups, they left the cups on the counter and quickly headed for the car. Suddenly it was all too clear what the good Samaritan truck driver meant earlier, with his parting remark. It had never dawned on any of them that they were traveling with anyone other than a friend and soldier. They were less than a mile from the diner when they saw the road sign that they were in Washington, D.C. Cooney, still very upset over the treatment his black friend received, was twice as upset over the fact that in our national capitol, a black man wearing a soldier's uniform could be denied a cup of coffee because of his color. It was difficult to understand and so very wrong.

After completing his tour of duty in February 1956, Cooney and his wife returned to New York City.

Cooney always had dreams of becoming a fireman, but a test was only made available every four years, so he had to sit tight and wait for the next one. After he was discharged from the Army, he tried a few different jobs, all the while checking the newspapers, looking for the notice that the Fire Department might soon be having another written test. Finally the notice appeared and on a Saturday morning in the spring of 1957, Cooney, along with 25,000 other applicants, took the written test. There were 4,000 applicants who passed the test and happily Cooney was one of them. Now he waited to be called for the next part of the test, which turned out to be an all-day competitive physical exam based on the entrance standards of West Point. Of those 4,000 applicants who took the physical exam, 2,000 passed the test, and Cooney was now on an official "Fireman List." It would take another year or so before Tom received his appointment notice, and in June of 1959 he was sworn in as a New York City fireman and issued lucky Badge #711.

While Cooney was a member of the fire department, the City witnessed some of the busiest fire duty times between the 1960s and 1970s. The reports of fires for the year of 1960 were 61,644, and by 1970 that number went up to 127,249 fires. In 1970 the fire department fought an average of 350 fires a day. From the years 1955–1966 there was an increase of 355 percent in false alarms and an 82 percent increase in fires.

CHAPTER 2

The next week Cooney started his fire department training and was assigned to a fire battalion in Brooklyn; every two weeks he would work in a different firehouse within the battalion until he was sent to the fire department school.

Cooney's first two-week assignment was with Ladder Company #102, in the Bedford-Stuyvesant section of Brooklyn, where he got some unexpected on-the-job experience. Near the end of his day shift, a phone alarm came in and everyone was dispatched to a nearby "working fire." As the junior man in the unit, Cooney was told to pull down the ceiling in the room adjoining the fire area to see if the fire was spreading. When he had nearly half of the ceiling down, the floor under him suddenly gave way, and plunged him ten feet into the basement below. Cooney said, "My lieutenant came rushing down in a panic after hearing the crash and was relieved to find me a little shaken, but otherwise unhurt, sprawled on top of a pile of junk. He said it was obvious that Badge #711 was working for me. He was also quite happy that since I was not hurt he would not have to face filing numerous reports about the incident. It certainly was a frightening way to get some on-the-job experience."

Cooney had heard earlier in the week that this particular building was ready to be torn down, but was still curious why the fireman referred to the alarm as a "working fire" when the call came in. They later explained that they recognized the address and knew the entire block was scheduled for the demolition crews. They also knew that the crews would be paid a higher hourly wage the next time they returned to work on the building if it was fire damaged, because it would now be considered an unsafe building.

The next two-week assignment was to Fire Squad #3, also located within the battalion in Brooklyn. The squad unit served several districts and responded to all their alarms. When they arrived at the fire, the chief in charge would determine whether the engine company or the ladder company needed the extra manpower and assign the squad members accordingly. When the fire was considered under control, the chief would then release the squad members to return to their firehouse. Cooney recalls one day, while working with the squad, the unit responded to a fire a few minutes after the start of the shift. They finished at that fire and were on their way back to the firehouse when they were diverted to a second location. Again, as they were on their way back, they were sent to a third location. This happened more than a dozen times that day and the squad did not get a chance to return to the firehouse until well after the shift ended. Cooney soon found out that this kind of schedule was a common occurrence and he left his two-week training with a healthy respect for the firemen in the squad units.

CHAPTER 3

It was now time for Cooney to begin actual training. With no central academy in existence then as there is now, Cooney's group started their first two weeks at an abandoned pier at the bottom part of Manhattan. Using an old fire engine, Cooney was taught how to stretch fire hoses and how to use different-sized nozzles. The group, however, soon learned that these hoses were old indeed and would never be fit to use for actual outside work; when full water pressure was exerted through the lines, the hoses would burst and drench the men thoroughly. Cooney and the other firemen soon learned to bring raincoats.

The next part of training involved the use of ladders and ropes—so it was back to the ladder school, which was located behind the engine company on 68th

Street in Manhattan. In back of the firehouse was a large courtyard where a variety of portable ladders and ropes were located for teaching how to make proper knots. There was also an aerial ladder on a fixed platform that was raised to the roof of a six-story building next to the firehouse.

"We were told that first day after lunch, everyone would have to climb the ladder all the way to the roof, and then we would put on life belts and would be shown how to lower ourselves from the roof down to the ground," Cooney recalled. "After lunch, three firemen were missing and never returned to the fire department school again.

"The aerial ladder didn't have any guide rails on the sides the way they do now, so it was a bit scary getting to the roof. I remember taking my time and trying not to look down. The next maneuver was no less scary. It required climbing over the side of the roof and, holding the rope, learning to lower yourself by sliding down the full six stories," he added. "When I reached the bottom I was relieved but felt a little bit more confident and was eager to try it again. The feeling of coming down on the roof rope, allowing you the ability to control how fast or slow you want to go down, gives you a great deal of confidence in yourself. I also think my two years of Army training made the fire department training school easier for me to complete.

"Near the end of our training at the ladder school, they showed us how to use a life net. We would be required to climb a fire escape one or two stories and jump into the net," Cooney explained, "but as one of the firemen trainees jumped into the net, he grabbed at his chest in pain and had to be taken to the hospital. It turned out his lung had collapsed, thus ending his career as a fireman.

"It should be noted," Cooney continued, "that a net is supposed to provide a bounce of sorts, and jumping and landing in a net is not as easy as it sounds. The key was to land on your butt in order to absorb the impact. This way you had a minimal chance of injuring yourself, so it was important to use the place with the most amount of cushioning."

When Cooney joined the fire department, he was measured for boots and a helmet. He chose the shorter rubber coat since he did not know whether he would be assigned to an engine or ladder company. The longer version was usually reserved for the engine man to keep him dry, and the shorter version for a ladder man to be more agile in climbing ladders. He happened to be assigned to a ladder company one day and on the way back from a run, he took his new coat off and hung it between the portable ladders on the side of the truck. As the truck was backing into the firehouse, his coat slipped off the ladder and the rear tiller wheels ran over the coat. When he retrieved the coat, he noticed two hooks that kept the front of the coat closed were broken. He wrote to the coat company requesting they send him four new hooks so he would have two spares readily available if needed. When they arrived, he opened the package only to find two of the four hooks were already broken. It made him laugh, then wonder just how much protection this coat would really provide.

After all the previous training, the firemen went to Roosevelt Island, where the city had a number of abandoned hospital buildings, at least one of which seemed ideal for the kind of training the new firefighters needed. In fact it was aptly named "the smokehouse," Cooney said.

"They put steel shutters on the hospital windows, which could be opened and closed. They would start a large fire in one of the rooms and then close the shutters to build up the heat and smoke inside. They would then put a rope dummy in one of the rooms and have ten of us go into the building in order to locate the dummy and bring it out to safety. But because of the intense heat and smoke, we would all be crawling back to the entrance door to try to get a breath of fresh air. When they finally opened the door, we all fell out on the ground, coughing and choking."

But times were beginning to change for the better when it came to equipping firemen. "They would give us a few minutes to rest and then they would tell us to put on a mask," Cooney explained further. "In those days, it was a face piece attached to a steel canister, which was made up of a charcoal filter, and that converted the smoke to breathable air. We were then sent back into the smoke room, but this time we could stand up and walk around the room, and we had no trouble finding the rope dummy and bringing it out.

"It should be noted, the mask was new to the fire department and the training crew was trying to convince the old-timers, who didn't believe in the mask, to wear one," Cooney said. "At this time, masks were really an entirely new concept; they were only used for mine fires. The only problem was that the canister filter would burn up, depending on how much work the man who was wearing it was doing, and then would suddenly stop functioning. The fireman would then be forced to retreat, but on occasion would be too far into the smoky building to safely reach an exit, resulting in a loss of life.

"Approximately two years later, those masks were removed and replaced with self-contained air tanks. The tanks and the plate were secured and made of heavy metal for durability, and added to the total weight a fireman had to carry. But it made a difference in putting out fires. Before the use of the mask, the old saying in the firehouse was 'You put the fire out, or you are carried out.' Many times entire companies would be lying out in the street after a fire and had to be taken to the hospital and treated for smoke inhalation and exhaustion. The masks have continued to improve through the years. Now they are made of a lightweight material and you have a longer period of time before you use up the air. When I was using the tanks, it would last for twenty minutes. Now it is up to forty-five minutes," Cooney said.

"We were told at the end of this training that two more recruits had decided the fire department was not meant for them. The instructors reasoned this type of extensive "smokehouse" training was necessary. They felt it was better to leave the fire department job here and now than take the chance of having someone actually get hurt working at the real thing.

"This finished our training at Roosevelt Island and our next step was classroom work, which was conducted in the fire department's garage facility, equipped with classrooms," Cooney continued. "It was an impressive building that was a full city block long, all open with just four rooms and a roof. There had to be at least eight fire engines and the same number of ladder trucks and chiefs' cars in the shop being repaired most any day of the week.

CHAPTER 4

Having completed his training, Cooney waited for his assignment. While he hoped to remain in Brooklyn, he was not unhappy to receive the news that an opening came up in Queens and he was assigned to Ladder Company #136. "I was now officially a 'probie,' being assigned to an actual unit and had some permanency," Cooney said. That new location actually responded to a large area in all four directions, some of it even touching Brooklyn a little bit, and going out to La Guardia Airport. But the company's workload, though well covered, wasn't very busy most of the time. Because of this, the firehouse and its equipment were kept very clean and in tip-top shape. "The entrance to the firehouse had a brass doorknob, and it had better be shining twenty-four hours a day, or else," Cooney recollected.

One of Cooney's earliest assignments in his new

house involved an apartment building during the holiday season of December 1959. Arriving at the site, heavy smoke was coming out of the building, and people were running to safety. The fire hydrant outside the building was blocked by a parked car, so the fireman had no choice but to break the car's two side windows to run the hose through in order to connect them to the hydrant. Cooney ran into the apartment and began to search the living room, without stopping for a mask. "When you first get there, you have to get inside quickly because timing can make a big difference. First responders usually do not wear masks for this very reason. The backup units, seeing they have a working fire to deal with, will put on masks and are then able to relieve the first due engine if needed. This was actually standard procedure," Cooney noted.

Then lying prone and crawling on his stomach, Cooney entered the bedroom and was able to open a few windows to relieve the heavy smoke that had built up inside. Meanwhile one of the other firemen spotted a woman in the bathroom lying prone in the bathtub. She was discovered as the open window allowed the smoke to lift. In the end, the fire was extinguished and the woman, after being given mouth-to-mouth resuscitation, was taken to the hospital where she was expected to recover.

The lieutenant said that in his many years on the job, he had never had a person found in a bathtub at a fire, so it was a learning experience for all of the firemen, to expect the unexpected. The cause of the fire was deemed to have originated from a live, dried-out Christmas tree that had come into contact with a frayed wire.

One night a few days after this fire, Cooney had another learning experience at a fire in the Rego Park section of Queens. The fire was in an apartment house on the fifth floor. The stretch for the engine company was a long one and it took longer than usual to get their hose lines to the fire site. The lieutenant took Cooney and the forcible entry man to the fire apartment, and because the door was secured by a few good locks, it took a few precious extra minutes to get the door opened. When they did, they were hit with heavy smoke and since they were the first due, they had no masks with them. The lieutenant told Cooney to use the fire extinguisher and try to contain the fire until the engine company hoses arrived, while he and the other fireman went on to search the three large bedrooms of the apartment. The fire had started in the living room and once again the cause was a burning Christmas tree. The engine company was able to get the water into the apartment and after a few minutes the fire was under control. The truck company got the windows opened and the heavy smoke began to lift in the apartment and then they made a terrible discovery. The man who lived in the apartment had tried to get out of the apartment and had almost made it to the front door before he was overcome by the smoke and collapsed. As he fell, his body became wedged next to a large stuffed chair and a corner wall. Due to the intense heat, heavy smoke, and being wedged against a wall by a stuffed chair, he was virtually invisible to the firemen until the smoke began to lift. He was immediately removed from the apartment to an ambulance, but unfortunately all attempts to revive him failed.

This was the second fire within a week where Cooney's unit was first due responder and he again witnessed the devastation that could be caused by a dried-out Christmas tree. It was, therefore, not unexpected when he made the decision that from then on he would only purchase artificial Christmas trees for his own home.

One particularly windy, bitter cold winter night, Cooney's unit responded to an alarm on Queens Boulevard, to a group of six attached two-story buildings with stores on the ground floor. When the first due engine company had arrived, the chief ordered them to take a hose line to the fire in the basement. Cooney's ladder company was instructed to check the offices on the second floor to search for people and see if the blaze had spread. After a thorough search, Cooney headed for the staircase and started to make his way down to the first floor. Just as he was turning into the first-floor hallway, there was a sudden and unexpected explosion in the basement that shook the building and knocked out the cinder-block walls. Cooney managed to back himself up onto the side of the staircase to avoid being hit by the full force of the blast and, while not a super-stitious man by nature, could not help but reach up and tap his #711 badge when he realized he suffered only singed eyebrows and minor facial abrasions in the mishap. The situation quickly became a multi-alarm fire and the number one priority was to rescue the trapped firemen in the basement and get them to the hospital. Fortunately none of them had life-threatening injuries and would recover.

In the meantime, the other firemen discovered the cause of the basement explosion was due to three leaking gas meters that were acting as blowtorches. How to shut off the gas supply became the next major problem. A call to the gas company resulted in only an approximate location of the line. When the rescue company arrived, they were instructed to dig up the street in front of the building in an attempt to locate the valves, but it was frozen solid and all attempts to turn them off failed.

By now the chief had obtained a copy of the building plans and located the gas line and valves. He then ordered Cooney's unit to take sledgehammers, axes, and roof saws to cut a hole in the front wall of the bank building. When the hole was large enough and the gas valves were visible, one by one the firemen took turns putting their arm through the hole to reach the valves and try to turn them. Due to the intense heat, each man could only leave his arm in the hole for a second or two, just long enough for one turn of the valves.

CHAPTER 4

Finally able to shut off the gas supply, the remaining engine companies were able to extinguish the rest of the fire. This was no easy task, since by now the first floor had totally collapsed into the basement, taking with it all of the bank's furniture and equipment.

There was evidence found at the site that indicated the fire may have been started by squatters who had gained entrance to the bank basement and lit a small fire to keep warm. As the flame grew larger and their attempts to contain it failed, they presumably fled the building in panic.

The intense heat in a confined area most likely caused the explosion. However, the true origin of the gas and the connection to the gas meters was never actually determined. Cooney recalls, "It was a combination of several different circumstances that made it such an unusual fire and makes it hard to forget."

The men were tired from their long, busy night and were wet and bitter cold standing on the running boards of the truck on the way back to the firehouse. They were silently pleased that the night had left no one seriously injured, including the firemen who were in the basement, and that they were able to save the stores on either side of the bank from major damage. Then someone looked up and caught sight of Cooney riding in the tiller seat, with his helmet and coat still covered in icicles, and looking very much like Jack Frost, and they all started to laugh and finally began to relax.

Cooney related an incident that happened a few weeks later, when the ladder unit was called to report to a high-rise building where a man was perched on the roof ready to jump. When they arrived, the lieutenant immediately went into the twenty-story building knowing the man on the roof was at a height beyond the aerial ladder's reach. The firemen below had no other choice but to get the life net ready. Cooney, along with the rest of the firemen, took the net to the area below where the man was sitting on the roof ledge. They did not open it for fear it would entice the man to make a move, and they all knew that a drop from that height would not end well for either the potential jumper or the firemen holding the net.

When the lieutenant got to the roof, a policeman was there and had already engaged the man in conversation to calm him down. The policeman offered him a cigarette and the man gladly accepted it. As the policeman was giving him a light, he and the lieutenant were able to grab the man and pull him back onto the safety of the roof. He was then taken to a hospital for treatment. When they returned to the firehouse, the firemen questioned their lieutenant on the proper procedure for the life net use and up to what height it would be safe to use. The lieutenant could not find any written standard procedures and said he would check with the battalion chief. The chief could not find any specific instructions on the life net usage either and passed the question on to Fire Headquarters. In the

CHAPTER 4

meantime the chief commended the ladder company for a job well done that evening and to keep up the good work. Apparently a official procedure had never been formally written. However, about nine months later, the Fire Headquarters issued a written policy stating the proper use of the life nets and under what circumstances they should and could be used.

While the work of a firefighter is serious business, there is always room for some levity. As mandated by Fire Headquarters, the deputy chief must visit each firehouse in his division on a yearly basis and conduct an inspection to ascertain that everything is in tip-top shape, with reference to cleanliness, maintenance, and equipment. "On one such inspection day," Cooney recalls, "we were all lined up, much like military style, standing at attention in full dress uniform. In front of each fireman was his equipment, boots, helmet, and turnout coat, laid out for the inspector to review. The deputy chief went down the row and when he came to the engine company lieutenant, who was an old-timer nearing retirement, he asked him to pick up his folded rubber coat. When he did, the coat cracked in two, falling into pieces due to a severe case of dry rot. As the coat cracked and fell, the other firemen, including the deputy chief, broke into laughter at their friend's misfortune. The lieutenant only used this coat for inspections and never expected the chief to ask him to pick it up. A few weeks later, the lieutenant was seen sporting a brand-new turnout coat."

CHAPTER 5

On another bitter cold night, this time in January 1961, as a heavy snow was blanketing the New York area, the watchman heard a first alarm go out around ten o'clock that a passenger airline had crashed on Rockaway Boulevard in Queens. The site was located in a large swamp-like area, and shortly a second alarm was sent in. The fire was under control within the next two hours, but this was not a normal fire situation. Since this was an airline, there were also 100 passengers involved who needed to be accounted for. More manpower was needed to help with the rescue and to search the site for anyone who might have been trapped or submerged in the swamp.

Back at Cooney's firehouse and all other surrounding Queens' firehouses, a request came in asking for one fireman from each house to be sent to the crash site to help in the search-and-rescue operation. Tom remembers his captain choosing him and saying, "As a new firefighter, this will be a good learning experience for you." As he was getting bundled up and ready to leave, one of the older firemen in his unit approached him and asked him to say hello to a Fireman Joe, a friend of his who was working at the fire site. He said, "Ask him how he likes fire duty." Tom looked at him a little puzzled, and the fireman went on to tell him that both of them had been members of the fire department band, which was recently disbanded, and the members were sent back to regular fire companies. Both of these two firemen had less than a year remaining before retirement.

Cooney arrived at the site and got to talk to fireman Joe , who was the friend he was asked to look for. The two men worked side by side through the long, hard night as the snow and cold wind swept over the area. Sadly, six passengers died as a result of the crash, and miraculously ninety-four survived. Most of them returned to the airport, while others never reported in or said a word to anyone; they just left the crash site and went directly home. Meanwhile, the firemen continued their search for the missing passengers. The search ended at 6 a.m., when the last passenger had finally been accounted for, and the firemen all returned to their respective firehouses.

At about 7:30 a.m., while Cooney was still trying to warm up with a cup of hot coffee, he heard that a second alarm had come in from the same Rockaway Boulevard area where he had just been. This time, however, the fire was at a private home, and the arriving fire company, including Joe, was told that two children were in one of the upstairs rear bedrooms. Hearing this, Fireman Joe quickly ran up the stairs to attempt a rescue, but never made it farther than the second-floor landing. He collapsed and died of a heart attack at the top of the stairs. Meanwhile the children were already safe, having found a way out of the building by themselves. The death of Fireman Joe hit Cooney hard. It was his first encounter with the death of a fellow fireman, and one he had just spent the last six hours working with. Unfortunately it would not be his last encounter with death.

One afternoon Cooney's firehouse received a phone alarm for an apartment fire that was only a few blocks away. Upon arrival, they discovered that the problem had occurred in a vacant apartment where the building superintendent was stripping the floors to prepare the apartment for a new tenant. The floor stripper required a lot of voltage, and the fuses tend to burn out quickly when using that kind of machinery. The superintendent tried to solve that problem by putting copper coins into the fuse box. Also, the type of material being used to loosen the wax was highly flammable and a spark from the machine caused the wax to ignite, creating a flash fire. The fire was extinguished quickly, and

CHAPTER 5

Cooney noticed his fire chief talking with the superintendent, who was asking for a cigarette. Cooney said he was surprised by the superintendent's request, and the chief noted it would very likely be the last cigarette he would ever smoke. The chief went on to explain, "Look at the superintendent's face. There are black marks coming from the man's nostrils. While the copper coins helped preserve the fuses, they also helped keep things running in an unintentional way. More specifically, the fuses have safety devices that are meant not to cause an overload, exactly what the coins were helping to create. That enabled a quick flash fire to result that went out almost as quickly as it started. However, in that short span, the man's lungs had been seared, and this very often can be fatal." The chief had called for an ambulance, but feared it might be too late since the superintendent was already experiencing excruciating pain and was crying out as the EMTs wheeled him away. They later learned that sadly the superintendent died on the way to the hospital.

At roll call in his firehouse one day, the captain of Ladder Co. #136 was in a fix because his regular driver was out sick. Driving a fire truck with men hanging onto the sides is not quite the same as driving a regular automobile or a smaller van or truck. Due to obvious size and bulk differences, it takes a learned skill to navigate when turning or maintaining lanes in emergency situations. So the captain was forced to call in a relief driver from another company. However, although the fireman who reported was a certified driver, his driving skills left much to be desired. This led the captain to post a notice informing the men there would be chauffeur training classes for the men on all shifts. Cooney took the training course and became a certified regular driver at the end of his second year on the job.

Maintaining a sense of humor is also important when you spend so much time dealing with many different personalities in close quarters, during long shifts, at the firehouse on any given day. For example: One day as everyone was returning from an alarm, the captain instructed one of his junior drivers to back the ladder truck into the firehouse. He did not think this would be a problem since there was a large wooden block on the floor to prevent the truck from going back too far. But not today. The young driver hit the gas pedal a little too much, causing the wheels of the tiller to go over the block and hit the inner rear wall with the end of the aerial ladder. The driver then slowly moved the truck forward and checked for damages. There were none, with the exception of a minor crack on two tiles on the back wall. Unfortunately, some practical joker in the firehouse decided to have some fun and placed a small metal gear at the base of the aerial control box near the center of the truck.

When the next shift arrived, someone spotted the metal gear near the control box. After several phone calls to the previous shift supervisors and careful examination of the fire truck, it was determined there was no visible damage to the truck, However, the lieutenant on duty still wasn't satisfied, so he ordered the firemen to take the truck outside, and for the next couple of hours, they raised the aerial ladder and turned it in every direction to ensure there was nothing wrong with it. It goes without saying that the men were not in a great mood the next morning when Cooney's shift came back to work. Just how the gear got on the truck or who put it there remains a mystery, although more than a few of the men could have ventured a good guess. Cooney says you need to have a sense of humor in a job like this, but will readily admit that not all practical jokes are funny.

CHAPTER 6

In the autumn of 1962, Cooney felt on top of the world, and why not? He had a wife, Edie, a one-year-old son, Edward, and a lovely apartment with four rooms on the first floor of a two-story house. He had a job he was happy with and life was good. One Sunday he took the family for a ride upstate to view the changing colors of fall, and they came across a sign that read, "lots for sale" in a lovely scenic neighborhood. After looking over the area and talking to the Realtor, they came back home, worked on their budget, and decided they could afford the $15.00 a month necessary to purchase a 50' X 120' parcel of land. Two years later, Cooney had a builder construct an unfinished interior building, known as a "shell house," on that lot, which he intended to finish himself. It turned out to be a smarter move than they anticipated at the time, because a few months later Cooney received notice that his apartment building had been sold and they would soon need to vacate their apartment. They attempted to find another suitable place to live, but couldn't find one the same size in their price range. Instead, they set out to find a builder who would finish the interior of their shell for them. The local lumber company recommended a very talented builder who not only was able to add an extension to the house, but was willing to work during the winter months so they could move into their home more quickly.

In March of 1964, when the Cooneys were finally ready to move to their new home, six of Tom's fellow firemen volunteered to help them move out of their old apartment. When they arrived at their new destination, they were surprised and delighted to find four other colleagues waiting to help move them in.

Now, Cooney had to put in for a transfer to a firehouse closer to their new home, so when an opening became available in Engine Co. #95, at the tip of Manhattan, he put in his transfer. As a member of Engine Company #95, Cooney and his new coworkers were taking turns with other engine companies in the area doing "night escort duty" for trucks coming into the city to deliver explosives to companies on Long Island and to the New England area. The firemen would meet the truck as it came off the George Washington Bridge late at night and escort them out of the city.

The fire department recommended taking the trucks over the Tri-borough Bridge (now known as the Robert F. Kennedy Bridge). However, this was a toll bridge and would have caused a major loss of revenue, as well as traffic congestion, in the event of an accident. Instead, the City decided the firemen should escort the trucks late at night, down Second Avenue through the sleeping neighborhoods to the toll-free Manhattan Bridge and out of the City. Some of the drivers of the explosive-laden trucks would be in a hurry to unload their cargo, and they would follow the engine company so closely, the firemen on the back step could feel the actual heat from the headlights of the truck. More than a few times, they had to climb up onto the hose bed because the truck followed so close behind them. Cooney laughs about it now, but continues to wonder, "If the fire engine ever had to stop short, I don't know what would have happened to us on the back step." Fortunately, it remains only a shuddering thought.

The Cooneys were now settled in their home with their son and new daughter, Linda. Tom thought a little cement patio would look good out front, but he had little experience in cement work, so he asked around the firehouse for suggestions. Luckily one of the firemen worked side jobs doing cement work and told Cooney to frame out the area for the patio and he would come up to help him. Several days later, after finishing a night tour, Cooney, his lieutenant, and two other firemen left the firehouse to do the patio.

When they arrived, the fireman who would be doing the cement work asked Cooney, "How much time do we have before the cement truck arrives?" Cooney told him about two hours. The fireman replied, "Good, because it will take me that long to fix your wooden frame." Amid much laughter he went ahead with the alterations and they were ready when the cement truck arrived. After a few hours the men were ready to take a lunch break while waiting for the cement to set. Tom's four-year-old son, Ed, asked if he could join them. Since the firemen were all wearing fire boots, they slipped him into a spare pair of boots too. Thinking the patio was finished, Ed stepped onto the cement with the heavy boots and to his surprise slowly began to sink. The firemen pulled Ed out of the boots, then retrieved the sinking boots and spent the rest of the day resetting the cement. It made for a fun story at the firehouse and a great "show and tell" story at nursery school for Ed.

By now Cooney had been a member of the NYC Fire Department for four years and split his time between engine and ladder companies. As an engine man, he was taught how to maintain and handle the heavy hoses, and how to carry the water-filled hoses into the building. The engine men would then have to quickly enter the building, locate the fire source, and extinguish the blaze. Meanwhile a specially trained engine man, known as the chauffeur, remained behind with the pumper to maintain the water pressure on the hoses.

The ladder man was trained to enter the fire building immediately upon arrival, conduct a search-and-rescue operation, and open the roof, doors, and/or windows to provide ventilation as needed. "I had been assigned to Engine Co. #95, but always felt I was better suited for the ladder company job," Tom notes, "so when I heard there was a opening in the ladder company in the same firehouse, I applied for a transfer and soon became a member of Ladder Co. #36. I had found my niche and would remain a truck man for the rest of my firefighting career."

CHAPTER 7

"Being in close quarters, working together for long hours, and the type of work we do, you come to rely on each other and become an extended family," Cooney says, "and like a family, we take care of one another if the need should arise." A case in point is the story of a fireman in Cooney's firehouse who had a wife and seven children and lived in one of the city's housing projects. Since he was having difficulty finding a larger affordable apartment for his family, he considered leaving the fire department after receiving a call from his brother with a job offer. The downside to the offer was that he would have to pack up his family and move to California. His brother worked as a union elevator installer and promised to get him a job and sponsor him until he could get his own union book. The fireman went to his superiors and asked if he could have a one-year leave of absence to try it out. He was turned down and now had to make a decision: stay in New York City and continue to struggle financially or take a big chance and go to California to start over in a new and better paying job. He left the fire department and moved the family 3,000 miles away to join his brother. Cooney and his fire mates continued to keep in touch with him, and all appeared to be going well in his new home and job. When they suddenly stopped hearing from him, they called to check on him and learned that his brother had died unexpectedly from a heart attack. He was now out of a job since he had lost the union protection his brother had originally afforded him. They asked him if he had any idea what he was going to do next. He said he wanted to come back to New York and try to get his job back with the fire department.

That's when the firemen in his old house got to work. They took up a collection every payday and sent him the money to help him get by. Then they began lobbying city fire officials and political leaders in the area to let their friend return home and come back to the fire department. It took some time, but eventually he was allowed to return to his job as a fireman. When he returned, he received a big welcome from his comrades, who had found him and his family a newer apartment to reside in and paid the first three months' rent for them.

This may be considered an unusual story, but Tom assured me almost every firehouse in the city has at least one similar story to tell of the men banding together to help a fellow fireman in need. Such a climate of brotherhood is indeed hard to find.

This type of commitment to one another is always there and never more visibly driven home than on that Wednesday night on October 18, 1966, when word of a four-alarm fire on E. 23rd Street in Manhattan was relayed across the city. The fire had begun in the basement of a five-story building that had a collection of art material, including wooden frames, lacquer, and paints. Within the hour, the fire was upgraded to a five-alarm status when the first floor collapsed, followed by the news that twelve firefighters had perished in the blaze. Cooney, who had been listening to the reports by department radio, went to the scene at the end of his shift, along with hundreds of other off-duty firemen from all sections of the City. When he arrived there at nine the next morning, Cooney immediately became part of a human assembly line of firemen who were sifting through every piece of the collapsed building in order to retrieve the bodies of the twelve firemen. Tom recalled, "When the body of a fireman was found, we were asked to leave the building and stand outside. It was an accepted procedure; as each fireman was carried out, we would all stand at attention and remove our helmets out of respect and as a tribute to our fallen brother." The funeral services were all held on the same day—four at St. Thomas' Episcopal Church, six at St. Patrick's Cathedral, and two in their respective hometowns of Westbury and Elmont—and were attended by thousands of firemen who came from all over the country.

Cooney explained that many times a small fire starts undetected after people have left work for the day, and it quietly erupts into a nightmare, such as this one clearly did. Yet, miraculously, one fireman was spared from joining his twelve fallen comrades when the ring on his finger caught on a fire nozzle and left him dangling above the collapsed floor until his buddies could pull him back to safety. Up to this time and for many years after, this particular event was the most devastating Tom and his fellow firefighters had ever been a part of, and it still remains fresh in Tom's memory. "You are always aware something like this is a possibility, but you pray it doesn't happen to you," Cooney recalled sadly. "But if it should, I always felt I could rest in peace knowing that my fire department buddies would be there for my family if they needed them."

Tom said a year or so later, a fireman from Engine Co. #37 named Ralph Feldman, known for being a talented artist and sculptor, decided to honor the memory of the fallen brothers by building a monument. Men from his unit and from Ladder Co. #40 helped by collecting burnt wooden beams, charred bricks, and scorched metal debris from actual fire sites. The end result was a thirty-foot charred beam with what appears to be a skeletal hand of steel at the cross section, giving the impression of a cross. It found a permanent home in the Cathedral of St. John Divine in Manhattan and remains there on display.

A tour Cooney recalls clearly was when he found himself boss for a day. He was working the day shift when the captain called him into the office and told him he had been designated acting chief for the day, and since Cooney was the senior man working in the truck unit, he would take over as acting lieutenant for the remainder of the shift.

Later that day the unit got a call to respond to an apartment fire. After a hose line had been stretched, the men entered the building, only to have the super-intendent inform them that two boys were still in the apartment where the fire was. As they entered the apart-ment, the firefighters were hit with heavy smoke and heat, forcing Cooney to get down and crawl along the floor in order to search for the boys. Cooney searched two rooms and when he reached a window, he opened it and took a breath of air. Seeing their tiller man ap-proaching the building, he shouted for him to bring a mask. As Cooney continued his search, he could hear someone in the apartment but was unable to locate him. When the tiller man entered the room with his mask on, Cooney let him continue the search, and shortly thereafter, they found the boy and brought him out to safety. He was then taken to the hospital, where he was treated and released. The older brother was also found hiding in a second room by another fireman in Cooney's unit. He too was hospitalized and recovered.

The fire was extinguished and everyone was satisfied with the results and with the rescue of the two boys. Everyone, that is, except Cooney, who began to question himself. He replayed the events of the day in his head and wondered why he was not able to locate the boy during his search. He knew he was a good fireman but felt he had more to learn, and maybe if he worked in a busier firehouse, he would gain the experience to become a better one. Anxious to test his theory, he chose a ladder company in Harlem and began his campaign for a transfer. It took nearly a year, but on Saturday, September 23, 1967, he officially became of member of Ladder Co. #30 in Harlem.

CHAPTER 8

On his first night shift after transferring to Ladder #30, Cooney and the unit responded to a fire in a two-story building that had been renovated and converted to a storefront church. Their unit was first due on this alarm. "My job," as Cooney recalls, "was to search the fire floor for anyone who might need to be evacuated." As the search continued, the smoke began to bank down, making it difficult to breathe without a mask. The dense smoke, combined with the many changes in the original floor plans, caused Cooney to become disoriented and lost while trying to make his way back to the other members in his unit. This was the first time since becoming a fireman that he actually had a sense of real fear. Meanwhile, another fireman, who was assigned to the roof, managed to break through the roof door, allowing the smoke in the building to lift. Cooney was then able to continue his search and safely find his way back to his lieutenant to report that there was no one found on the fire floor or in the rest of the building.

After the fire was out and the units returned to the firehouse, Cooney was in the house watch office when he caught a glimpse of a red object pass by the office door. Apparently, the brake on the fire engine was not properly set, and it caused the engine to roll. It came to a stop by hitting the firehouse door and bending the door track in the door channel, making it impossible to operate the door. All three fire units would now be unable to respond if a fire alarm should happen to come in. Cooney and two other members of the truck company grabbed some tools and immediately started working at bending the door track open again. There was a lot of banging noise and soon there was a call from the lieutenant upstairs wanting to know what all the racket was about. Cooney told his officer what had happened and what they were doing. The lieutenant asked him if he thought he could fix the problem. Tom assured him they would be able to take care of it. It took about an hour for the three men to repair the bent track, allowing the door to once again open freely. All three units were now again available to respond when the next call came in. There were no further questions or comments from the lieutenant for the rest of the shift. He had been assured the matter would be taken care of properly and he was satisfied. He never referred to the incident again.

After that night, Cooney, who already was comfortable with his decision to transfer to Harlem, felt at home and knew he would be happy there.

His new company was located at 133rd Street and Lenox Avenue and had been built in the early 1960s as a replacement for a much older firehouse on 135th Street. The first floor had an office for the house watch, a small room for a TV, a bathroom, and a kitchen. The second floor had a locker area, a bathroom, a sleeping area, and an office. The only thing wrong with this arrangement was that the firehouse was occupied by three companies—an engine company, a truck company, and a squad unit—and the kitchen was way too small to accommodate them at any one time. Worse yet, the stove that the City had provided was always in need of repair and the sink leaked. The three companies got together and decided to enlarge the kitchen area and replace the stove and sink. That meant opening the kitchen wall and moving the clothes racks to the rear of the first floor in order to use that area for the new stove and sink. When everyone was satisfied with the new layout, they all contributed money and went ahead with the project.

Unfortunately when Fire Headquarters got word of this, they were furious that the men had completed the project without the proper permission and permits. They sent word to the captain of the engine company that he would be brought up on charges. Several weeks later, two chiefs arrived at the firehouse, and everyone feared the charges were forthcoming. Instead these chiefs had brought a guest chief from Los Angeles with them just to show off the renovations the firemen had made with money out of their own pockets. All the chiefs were impressed and quite pleased with what the firemen had accomplished, and there was no mention of any charges. After they left, Cooney's captain pulled him aside and told him that the handball court out back, which was never used much, would make a fine sitting room. But, that's another story...

While they were completing the rear sitting room, it came to the firemen's attention that a nearby building was being demolished and the bricks were for sale. Some of the firemen thought those bricks might make a perfect facing for the old cement handball court wall at the rear of the room. So, after a discussion among the three companies, they agreed to chip in and purchase a truckload of used bricks. The truck captain knew of a fireman in another firehouse who was a brick layer before he joined the fire department, and made arrangements to have him detailed to our firehouse. He stayed for a month and helped put up the brick wall. Just like the renovations to the kitchen and sitting room, the work was done a little at a time, during the day shifts in between fire runs. Cooney remembers helping to put up the roof beams and straddling the outside cement wall while cutting off the ends of the beams with the roof saw. There were times after a day tour he felt tired enough to fall asleep on the ride home and would have to stop for an extra strong cup of coffee.

The renovations were completed and the men were just beginning to enjoy the results of their efforts when a directive arrived from headquarters. The captain was informed that the entire squad unit would be transferred to the South Bronx, due to a recent sharp increase in their fire calls. No one was happy when they heard the news. After all the time, effort, and money the units had contributed to improve the conditions at the firehouse, now not everyone would remain there to enjoy it. Also, after working together during the construction process, the men among the three units had formed a closer bond than usual. However, there was an immediate need for the squad unit in the South Bronx, so despite impassioned pleas from everyone involved, the move was made. "We all missed them," Cooney still reflects today. "They were a great bunch of guys."

About a year later, the remaining companies were further saddened when they learned that one of their buddies from the transferred squad unit, as well as a fireman from a truck unit, had died in a terrible accident. The accident occurred the night the squad unit responded to a third-alarm fire in the Bronx, at a lumber yard located next to a railroad line. The fire was put out and the firemen were packing up their equipment when, by accident, their metal ladder hit a live power line and they were killed instantly. Tragically, the firemen were unaware that the power, which had previously been turned off, had already been restored to the line. Their buddies in the Harlem firehouse were all deeply stunned and shaken by the news and came to realize that in this job, as well as in life, nothing should be taken for granted.

The construction of the rear room and the brick wall were now complete when a new opportunity knocked on their door. The City made plans to widen their street by cutting and trimming the sidewalks on either side. The contractor in charge approached the firehouse with a request. He asked, when the time came, if he could leave his machines and equipment in the firehouse parking lot in order to protect the equipment and save the extra expense of hiring a night watchman. He was told it would not be a problem. The firemen then asked him if there was any asphalt left over when his job was finished, would he consider giving it to them for their parking lot, and he said he would.

In the meantime the back of the parking lot was still in need of a retaining wall, so the firemen got busy constructing a wooden form, and now all that was missing was the cement. As luck would have it, there was also a contractor working on sidewalk repairs in the area, and he too agreed to give the firemen any leftover cement. When the call came that the cement truck was on the way, the men lined up behind the forms ready to evenly distribute the cement. But the driver was anxious to get home and in a hurry to get rid of the cement and poured it too fast, causing the form to start giving way. Cooney was in the center, shoveling as fast as he could, when

CHAPTER 8

it happened and was soon covered with cement. Just then the fire alarm rang and everyone jumped on the trucks to respond, including Cooney, who had no time to free himself of the cement on his clothes. When they arrived at the fire site, the chief in charge took one look at Cooney sitting in the tiller seat all covered in cement, shook his head, and said, "I don't think I want to know anything about this." The fire was extinguished and the units returned to the firehouse to finish the work on the cement wall, which remains standing to this day.

A few weeks later the street widening was completed and the contractor was ready to make good on his promise. The captain asked Tom to please take care of the workers while they were outside doing the job. The next day Tom came in with bagels and rolls for breakfast, and when it was time for lunch included the twenty men in on the meal. Later that afternoon the foreman came to Cooney and said his work crew was thirsty from working in the heat and suggested some beer as their choice of beverage. As the men continued to work, Tom complied with trips to the store. When the day was over and the work crew was finished, the firemen were surprised by what they saw. It appeared the workers were so taken by the hospitality and generosity of the firemen, they paid them back by doing more than they had promised. Instead of just pouring leftover asphalt on a small section of the lot, as expected, they paved the entire parking lot, making enough room to park twelve cars.

CHAPTER 9
BITS AND PIECES

Most firemen find it vital to have a sense of humor to deal with some of the darker aspects of the job. But their humor is not always understood or appreciated, as was the case in the following incident.

Among the men in Tom's firehouse was a group of men who enjoyed taking fishing or hunting trips. When they returned from these trips, they would usually bring back to the firehouse various fish or deer meat for everyone to enjoy. However, preparing the deer meat before it is ready to be made into a meal can be a very messy and bloody affair. One day, as a few firemen were finishing the preparation process, they noticed the blood had begun to spill out from under the firehouse door onto the sidewalk out front. A fireman was quickly stationed outside to advise anybody passing by where the blood was coming from. Instead, when a couple did pass by, the fireman commented loudly, "You know *he's* not going to pull any more false alarms!" The couple looked at him and ran down the street. The lieutenant overheard the remark and ran after the frightened couple to try to explain that it was only meant as a joke and was indeed in bad taste. He also convinced them that a call to the police was unnecessary. Then he offered them some of the venison meat to take home for their dinner, which they accepted reluctantly.

On one particularly busy Friday night, the companies were out on runs continuously from roll call at 6 p.m. until well after 10 p.m. By then, the thought of food played heavily on the minds of the hungry firemen. Since there had been no time to cook a meal, the captain asked Cooney to go to the local Chinese restaurant and bring back enough food for everyone. He said the place had good food, was inexpensive, and usually gave firemen a discount. So the order was placed and Cooney went to get it. When they gave him the bill, he found himself well short of the cash needed to pay for it. One by one, some of the order was removed from the bag until he had enough money to pay for what was left. Cooney felt his face getting redder by the minute, while some of the patrons found the circumstances very amusing. When Cooney finally returned to the firehouse, he told the captain what happened and asked him when he had last been to this restaurant. The captain apologized and admitted it had been a couple of years and the prices probably went up when the new owners took over.

The men had just started to eat when an alarm came in about a fire at the rear of a store on 124th Street that was quickly spreading to the front of the store on 125th. Cooney's job was to cut a large hole in the roof in the middle of the store to help vent the fire and prevent its spread. At the time the company roof saw was in the repair shop, so he had to cut the roof the hard way, by using an ax and six-foot hook, which takes longer. Meanwhile another member of the unit had come up to the roof to assist Tom, and it became clear that the roof had a lot of bounce to it and was getting soft. This was a sure sign for them to get off the roof quickly. They had just reached the adjoining roof when the front window of the store blew out, sending glass and bricks out into the street. The debris also hit the fire engine that supplied the water to the hoses of the fire units inside the building. The fire was now upgraded to a fourth-alarm fire. It took another hour before the fire was pretty much under control and the unit was told to take a coffee break, courtesy of the Salvation Army.

Cooney was just about to take a sip of his coffee when a man came running up to him to report a fire in a hotel room right down the street. Tom sent him to the corner to pull the lever on a fire alarm box, while he ran down to the hotel. What he found was a mattress fire in one of the rooms. He managed to put it out with his fire extinguisher and by using some from the hotel as well. When the other fire unit arrived, Tom went back up to his company—just in time to hear the chief say break time was over and everybody was to head back to work. So much for being a good Samaritan.

On more than one occasion after a busy night tour, sometime around 7 a.m., as the firemen would be looking forward to the end of their shift, the house watchman would call for the engine and truck. When they got to the first floor, they could smell burning garbage, and outside the firehouse would be a city garbage truck with heavy smoke pouring out of the back of it. The engine men would then get a length of hose, and the truck men would open the side door of the garbage truck in order to hose down the burning garbage. However, this did not always work, so the sanitation driver needed to raise the back of the truck and dump the entire garbage load so it could be spread out and hosed down. When the fire was out, all of the wet, burnt garbage now had to be shoveled back into the truck. Ah yes, fond memories of another end to a night tour in Harlem.

CHAPTER 10

Firemen receive credit at work for a job well done, but rarely does anyone take notice of some of the outrageous efforts necessary to get to work on time during inclement weather. Cooney jokingly recalls one such arduous trip. As part of his routine before retiring for the night, he would watch the news and check the weather forecast. One winter night, he took notice that there was a chance of heavy snowfall being forecast for the area. So he set the alarm for 4 a.m., and the next morning, when he saw the snow had already started to accumulate, he quickly got dressed and left for work. The road travel was down to a slow crawl, with snow falling faster than the plows could handle. But the situation got worse and time was passing. As Cooney got closer to the City, the storm changed from snow to heavy rain and high winds. When Cooney finally arrived at the

George Washington Bridge, he was informed that due to the extreme high winds he would not be permitted to cross in his Volkswagen bus. Cooney found a police officer, told him he had to report to work, and showed him his fire badge. The policeman then came up with a plan. He stopped two large tractor-trailers and got permission for Cooney to drive his Volkswagen between them, in a convoy sort of fashion. The policeman wished him luck and sent them on their way. It took five hours and ten minutes before the entire trek was over and Cooney finally reached his destination.

Cooney had just arrived at the firehouse and was still changing into his fire gear when the alarm sounded and they were on their way to St. Charles Borromeo Church. A fire had flared up in the middle of the church, above the lights. The firemen attempted to get under the roof and into the crawlspace. However, the crawlspace proved to be too narrow to accommodate their masks, and without them the fire and smoke drove them back. Then, Cooney and another fireman were told to go to the adjacent roof of the rectory building where the priests resided. Their job was to pull a hose line, with a heavy multiversal nozzle attached, up to the roof of the rectory. However, with the continuous heavy rain and high winds, it was very difficult for them to pull the heavy equipment onto the roof. That's when Tom's partner, Bill, spotted a man near the roof entrance and yelled at him to move his "hindquarters" (albeit not exactly in those nice words) to come over and help them, and he quickly did, without hesitation. It became necessary to surround the church and use all the tower ladders and fire engines to pour water onto the roof and into the church. But the storm winds were so strong that sometimes the water did not even reach the roof. The units continued to shoot heavy water streams at the fire, and eventually it was extinguished. Unfortunately, the church roof was completely destroyed and would take the better part of two years to be replaced. However, everyone was happy they were able to save the church.

Before they left, Tom and his partner were told to go downstairs to get some hot coffee from a man who was handing out beverages. They were surprised when they recognized the man as the person who came to their aid on the roof. But surprise quickly turned into embarrassment when he smiled and introduced himself as the new pastor of the church. Cooney's buddy immediately began apologizing for the foul language he'd used on him earlier. The pastor graciously assured him that no harm had been caused by his words and all was forgiven. The pastor may have forgiven him, but his fire buddies took great pleasure in teasing him about the incident for many, many months.

One day shift when Cooney reported to the firehouse, he found that the ladder, engine, and squad units from the night shift were all still out at a fire. They had responded to an early morning alarm in an apartment house that nearly cost a Ladder #30 fireman his life. When the units arrived, the fire had already started to spread from the first to the second floor. The roof man from Ladder #30 came down the fire escape from the roof and entered the top floor apartment when it suddenly burst into flames. The roof man was unable to leave through the interior, and the exit to the fire escape now was cut off. He called for help on his radio. The engine company on the first floor tried to move their hose line up the staircase, but they were driven back down by the intense fire. The truck lieutenant and another man from the truck went up to the roof to try to help the trapped fireman, who was now hanging out of the kitchen window because of the rapidly spreading fire. The lieutenant attempted to reach the fireman with a six-foot hook to pull him up to the roof, but that did not work. Then the trapped fireman told his lieutenant that he was unable to hold on any longer, and fell five stories into a pile of garbage. The fireman was still alive when the squad unit reached him, and they rushed him to the hospital, where he remained for several weeks. He later said he believed the clothesline he hit as he was falling to the ground helped to slow him down and played a part in his survival. However, due to his multiple injuries, he was forced to retire from the job.

Cooney sadly notes that a short time later, they did lose a member of the unit from Ladder #30. Ironically, it was the same fireman who assisted the lieutenant in the trapped fireman in the apartment blaze a month earlier. Tom recalls that they were working at a fire, and when the fire was out and everyone was leaving the building, the fireman turned to his buddy and said, "Come on, let's go home." Those were the last words he had a chance to say before collapsing and falling to the ground. He had suffered a heart attack and died instantly. Ladder #30 lost a good man and a great fireman that day. He was also a widower and a dad who left behind six children.

CHAPTER 11

When you are in a city like New York, you have everything at your disposal. Good restaurants, beautiful museums, great ballparks, and entertainment. But with so many diversified people living there, you also have your share of crime and unrest. In the early 1960s, the NYFD began experiencing problems in certain areas of the City. Reports of objects being thrown from rooftops at the fire trucks, while they were responding to alarms or returning to the firehouse, became all too frequent. To prevent further injuries, the fire department began installing wooden covers over the rear fire engine back steps and the roof of the tiller wheel compartment. This added protection came into play and saved Cooney from serious injury when riots broke out after the death of Dr. Martin Luther King in April 1968.

By now Cooney had been in his new company for

about six months. He was surprised to learn that this company responded to 2,281 alarms, of which 1,211 were working fires. In the next eight years that Cooney worked in L-30, the number of alarms would go up to 3,123 and working fires to 1,774. Then came the evening of April 4, 1968, when newscasters were busy informing the nation of Dr. Martin Luther King Jr.'s assassination in Memphis, Tennessee, earlier in the day. Cooney heard the news at home and attempted to call his firehouse, but was unable to reach anyone because the men were already busy at a fourth-alarm fire on Lenox Avenue, where an entire row of stores was ablaze. When Cooney finally reached an officer at the firehouse, he was told to get a good night's sleep and be ready for anything on his next shift. The situation continued to get worse. By nightfall, five other truck units had to be called in from other boroughs to cover the Harlem area, and all were directed to ongoing fires even before they reached the firehouse. Some of them came from as far away as Coney Island. The following week, most of the stores in Harlem had been broken into and/or burned—even stores that had signs out front informing everyone that the owner was black. Many of the stores had apartments above them, and even though the fires were put out quickly, those families who lived in them still lost their home and all their belongings.

On Cooney's next night tour, his unit responded to two more major fires that kept them out most of the night. Returning to the firehouse from the second call, Cooney was up in his usual spot, driving the tiller wheel, and remembers hearing a loud crash. The next thing he knew, his face was pinned down on the tiller steering wheel as his comrades were frantically pulling crushed plywood off his head. They soon discovered that some hoodlum had dropped a cinder block from the top of a building onto the truck as the men were passing by. The newly installed wooden roof had saved Cooney's life, and miraculously he escaped with only a bad headache and a black eye that night. Cooney was wearing his helmet when the accident happened, and his lieutenant happened to take notice of his badge number. Each time he would pass by Tom the rest of the evening, he would remind him how his Badge #711 proved to be lucky for him once again. Tom remembers rubbing his sore head and thinking he couldn't agree more. About a week or so later, the madness began to settle down. But unfortunately by then, there was not a store to be found that had escaped the chaos, so people living in Harlem were forced to travel to the Bronx just to purchase a bottle of milk.

Cooney recalls another aspect of the job that was difficult to deal with, and never got any easier: the loss of life, and the circumstances that led up to the loss. One night Cooney and his company responded to a fire on the second floor of a vacant building. The lieutenant sent him downstairs to pull down the ceilings that were under the fire floor. As he was pulling them down, Cooney's hook caught on something and would not budge. All his efforts to free the hook proved futile, so he took his flashlight and shined it up into the ceiling, hoping to find the cause of the problem. It took only a few minutes before he realized what was happening. His hook had become entangled in the clothing of a dead man's body, which had been left on the floor above. As was the procedure, the police were called and a preliminary examination was made. It appeared the man had been brutally murdered and his body placed on top of a pile of debris, then set on fire in order to hide the crime.

As the firemen were getting ready to place the body in the body bag, the sergeant in charge asked Tom to wait a minute while he called his two new young officers upstairs to view the scene. When they arrived, he told them to take a good look at the body and pile of burned debris, and remember what they saw. He said he wanted this to make an impression on them so they would be extra careful and aware of their surroundings while out on patrol. Shortly thereafter, the people from the coroner's office arrived and took away the body, while Tom and the others gathered up their equipment and returned to their firehouse, trying to get the images out of their head.

Tom may not be able to remember the exact location of this alarm, but unfortunately still vividly recalls the scene. The unit was responding to an apartment fire and as they were pulling in, Tom, from his tiller seat, spotted a woman at a window. She was desperately trying to break through the steel gate attached to the front of her window in an attempt to reach the fire escape. Tom and another fireman jumped off the truck and ran up to her apartment. But before they could reach her, she was overcome by heavy smoke and died a short time later. To this day, he can still picture the woman in that window.

Another memory he would like to erase is the afternoon his unit was called to investigate the strong odor of smoke in a building. When they arrived, they noticed smoke coming from one of the apartments, and they were able to enter it from the fire escape. They discovered the cause of the odor was from heavy smoke coming from a mattress that had burned down to the steel coils. They also discovered two small young boys, huddled together in the corner of the room, both dead from smoke inhalation. The mother of the two young victims was not home. She was down the street at the local tavern. It was later determined that the two boy were left unattended and, more than likely, occupied their time by playing with matches. Tom found dealing with tragedy and death was always difficult and hard to accept, but dealing with the needless loss of life of young children is harder still. "Scenes like that stay with you forever."

CHAPTER 12

One bitter cold night, Cooney and his unit responded to an apartment building that had filled with smoke. It didn't take long before the cause of the smoke became clear. The superintendent conceded that the smoky building could be his fault. Earlier in the day he had emptied hot coals from the furnace and shoveled them onto the floor to allow them to cool before putting them into trash cans. That was his daily procedure. However, the superintendent then left the building for a short period, and while he was gone a new load of coal, about ten tons worth, had been delivered and ended up on top of the hot coals. As a result, the pile of coals started to smolder and smoke started to filter through the building.

The chief had his engine company wet down the coals, but this approach wasn't doing the job. Next they considered flooding the basement with water. This would stop the smoldering, but would likely ruin the boiler, leaving the tenants without heat in the freezing temperatures while the boiler was being repaired or replaced. The engine men certainly did not want to be responsible for that, so they quickly eliminated that option. It was then decided that the truck company would have to resolve the problem the hard way, by shoveling the coal from one storage bin to another bin next to it, until they could reach the hot coals. The long, grueling process took about four hours to complete. With the new coals moved to another bin, the hot coals were finally exposed and the engine company could now put out the smoldering fire. The firemen all returned to their firehouse tired, hungry, and sore, looking more like coal miners than firemen.

It was common practice for a fireman or two to cook a meal for lunch during a day shift. One payday the units decided to splurge a little and picked up some spareribs from the local meat market on 125th Street. They asked Tom, who often did the cooking, if he would prepare them for lunch. The ribs were just about ready when an alarm came in. When they arrived at the alarm site, they could find no fire or smoke in the building. After a careful search the firemen returned to the firehouse to enjoy their ribs, only to find that the ribs had mysteriously disappeared. Apparently, someone smelled the ribs cooking, placed a false alarm to get the firemen out of the firehouse for a little while, then came in and stole their lunch. Cooney and the others had to settle for franks and beans instead. It was a sad and expensive lesson to learn—that not all of their neighbors were friendly.

Another time, the firehouse had a covering lieutenant assigned for the day, but from the time he arrived, the department phone rang repeatedly just for him. This continued until lunchtime, and during the meal, Cooney decided to ask him what made him so popular. The lieutenant told them that his last assignment was in Staten Island and while he was there, his company responded to a brush fire. While the firemen were putting out the fire, the wind suddenly changed and picked up and changed direction, spreading the fire quickly to other buildings. It became a multi-alarm fire that destroyed about 100 homes and left hundreds of people homeless. Since he was the first arriving engine company, it was his responsibility to fill out all the fire incident reports. He said he hoped to be able to finish them before he made captain.

Cooney and his firehouse had a decent relationship with residents on the block (with the exception of the lunch thief) but one morning at the end of a night shift, a fireman was surprised to find a broken bottle had cracked his car windshield in the parking lot. Over the next couple of weeks, more cars showed isolated signs of damage until one morning Cooney found a steel pipe sticking out of his car roof. After that, every night, the firemen took turns watching the apartment building behind the lot, to see if they could pinpoint where the thrown objects were coming from. When they were finally able to locate the exact apartment, a few firemen went up to visit the tenant and announced themselves by banging loudly on the door. When the suspect opened the door, the firemen rushed in and asked why he was throwing objects out of his window at their cars. The man replied that a month ago there had been a fire in the apartment above his, and when the water was used to put it out, his apartment had water damage, and now he was getting even. The firemen said they were sorry, but water has a natural tendency to flow downward. The suspect would not listen to them and continued to rant. So in an attempt to get his attention, the firemen picked him up and held him out of his window and told him that if any more things were thrown out of his window, they would return and possibly do the same to him. That logic he understood, and from then on he caused no more problems.

Ladder 30 had just returned to the firehouse when the firemen noticed a man, dressed in a suit, in their parking lot taking measurements. They approached the gentleman and asked if they could help him. He said that he worked for the City and his job was to check out all vacant lots owned by the City, to see if any would make a suitable park. He was delighted when he came across this parking lot because it was already paved, and he thought with a few poles it could turn into a small basketball court. He did not consider the fact that a park at this site might be impractical and dangerous for the children, with three large fire vehicles coming and going all day long. The firemen were not pleased either, considering all the money they had just laid out putting up a fence at the front of the parking lot, plus all the time and labor they put into trying to keep their belongings safe while they were out on fire calls. So they put their heads together and decided to do something about it.

One of the firemen was sent down the street to speak to four of the local kids who were usually standing around. He asked them if they wanted to make some ice-cream money, and they, of course, said yes. They asked what they had to do. He pointed out the man in the suit and told them to tell him something that would scare him out of the neighborhood, but not to touch or harm him. They laughed and said okay. A few minutes later the man was seen running down the block, in the opposite direction of the firehouse. The man never came around to check the lot again and the fireman never asked the boys what they said to him to make him run.

Another Harlem tour that lingers in Cooney's thoughts began with an unusually quiet start to a summer night shift. It was the kind of eerie silence that everyone knew would be too good to last. Sure enough, at two o'clock in the morning, the silence was broken by an alarm that came in for a fire at a store on 125th street. The first due engine and truck companies were already engaged fighting the store fire, when Cooney's second due ladder company 30 and engine company 59 arrived. The chief directed them to check out the adjoining laundromat to check if the fire had spread to that store. When the two units entered the building, the dense smoke had already billowed its way down to the floor so they had to crawl their way to the center of the store. The truck members made an attempt to put a hole in the suspended ceiling with their six foot hooks, but found the ceiling beyond their reach. Cooney spotted a row of washing machines and climbed on top of them, thereby enabling him to reach the ceiling, poke a hole in it and determine if the fire had spread. As he was retracting his hook, it caught onto the metal support holding the suspended ceiling in place. Within seconds the ceiling came crashing down, hitting Cooney and knocking him to the floor. As the ceiling continued to fall, fireman from both companies were buried under the falling tiles, dust and debris. The chief gave the order to evacuate the store, making sure everyone was accounted for, and to check that no one had sustained any serious injuries. Coney was shaken and had multiple bruises, but was otherwise unhurt. The two companies then returned to help put out the fire that had spread to the laundromat. An hour later, when the fire was under control, the chief told the fire units to take a ten minute break before, "taking up" and returning to the firehouse. The engine lieutenant walked over to

Cooney and asked if he was the firemen on top of the washing machines. Tom said he was . The Lieutenant commented that he thought for sure, with a hit like that, I would be on my way to the hospital by now. Tom assured him he was not seriously hurt and would be fine. As the Lieutenant turned to leave he spotted Tom`s helmet and badge #711 and remarked, "Looks as if that number is really working for you". Tom remembers nodding and thinking the very same thing himself.

CHAPTER 13

Working a day shift at the firehouse in Harlem was always interesting. One day during the 1970s, Cooney was sitting at the watch desk when two police officers came into the firehouse asking to speak to the truck officer. They were getting ready to make a raid on the apartment building on the street behind the firehouse and asked if they could borrow the firehouse's heavy sledgehammer for a couple of hours. The truck officer gave them the hammer, and two hours later, while the firemen watched from the rear window of the firehouse, the police conducted their raid. People were running in all directions, coming out of doors, others climbing out of windows and fleeing down fire escapes, all trying to elude the police who were chasing them. It almost looked like a scene from an old silent movie, only this was real life. Several were caught and arrested for drug possession and distribution. For Cooney and the rest of the firemen, it was another interesting day on the job in Harlem.

Another night when Cooney was on duty, a phone call came in reporting a fire in the apartment house behind the firehouse, in the same building where the drug raid was conducted just a month ago. The truck officer and Cooney entered the building and headed for the rear apartment on the second floor. As they entered the apartment, the heavy smoke forced them to drop to the floor and crawl to continue their search for anyone who might be in the apartment. The lieutenant went in one direction and Cooney in another. Soon the lieutenant called out that he had located an unconscious male. Cooney started back to assist the lieutenant when he found a woman. He was carrying her out of the smoky apartment when he noticed that her hands and feet were tied. Cooney tried to revive her, but she was unresponsive. As the smoke began to clear, the lieutenant noticed that the man he found was also bound hand and foot. It appeared as if the man and woman had been murdered and the apartment was set on fire to cover up the crime. When the police arrived they were able to identify the bodies and later commented that they weren't surprised this had happened; both victims were known drug dealers, and this was probably a drug transaction that went very wrong.

Cooney is fond of remembering some of the good relationships he and other firemen had with the people living on 133rd Street in Harlem. In particular one feisty lady in her fifties, who wore the scars on her face of her hard life on the streets, was affectionately known as Mama Lew. She would make it her daily business to keep a watch on the firehouse when the men were summoned to an alarm. One day two men approached the back of the empty firehouse and began helping themselves to some supplies and miscellaneous tools. Fortunately Mama Lew spotted them. She grabbed a broom and began swinging it at them, chasing them out of the firehouse and down the street. A passing police car saw Mama Lew in pursuit and apprehended the two men. After that incident, Cooney recalls, Mama Lew was made an honorary member of the firehouse.

A few weeks later Cooney brought Edie, Ed, and infant daughter Linda to the City to visit relatives, but stopped first at the firehouse to pick up his paycheck. As he and his family were getting out of the car, a woman approached them and whisked the baby from Mrs. Cooney's arms, leaving her stunned and shaken. Cooney immediately recognized the woman and quickly introduced Mama Lew to his wife. Mama Lew apologized for frightening Mrs. Cooney and said when she saw the beautiful blond, blue-eyed baby, she thought she looked like an angel and just wanted to hold her. There was no harm done and all was forgiven. From then on, whenever Cooney was working and saw Mama Lew, she would ask about his beautiful angel and ask when he was bringing her back for a visit. For many more years Mama Lew held her honorary member status at the firehouse, and upon her death, the firemen took up a collection from former and present firemen who knew her, and gave her a proper funeral and final resting place.

CHAPTER 14

At one point, firemen across the City were seeking a new contract and, as such, agreed to have a designated civilian ride along with them in order to help conduct an independent study evaluating how the men fought fires and did their jobs. One night at roll call, the men were notified that for the next two weeks, an appointed civilian would be riding with their company. The Ladder 30 truck was old and had an oil-burning problem, and when the truck was responding to an alarm, it smoked so bad that it looked like it was on fire. After two runs, the civilian called the chief and told him he could not continue riding on the truck because of all the smoke. So it was decided the civilian would ride with the chief.

An hour later an alarm came in, and when Ladder 30 arrived at the fire scene, the first due engine and truck were already in the building fighting the heavy fire in the second-floor apartment. Cooney was the tiller man and as he was climbing down from the tiller wheel, a crowd of civilians started to yell about a lady on the top floor of the building who was in trouble. Cooney reported to the driver, and they put up the aerial ladder to the window where the lady was. As Cooney began his ascent up the ladder, he could see that there was now water coming out of the fire apartment windows, and the fire seemed close to being under control. When he got up to her window, he could hear the fireman entering her apartment. Tom saw that the woman was old and frail and did not think she would do well on the aerial ladder, so he spoke with her and told her to stay by the window and the fireman would take care of her. Cooney started back down the aerial ladder amid murmurs from the crowd below who assumed he had left the woman alone and in trouble. The chief asked Cooney what happened up there, and Cooney told him that the woman was in no danger since there were firemen already in her apartment who said they would take care of her. He also told the chief that he thought taking her down the aerial ladder would have caused the woman unnecessary harm and further trauma. The chief then explained the circumstances to the bystanders, who were greatly relieved. The civilian guest wanted to know who made the decision, and Cooney told him he did. The chief added that experienced truck men like Cooney made decisions like this all the time.

CHAPTER 14

Cooney was a little apprehensive over whether the civilian guest would find it necessary to include this in his evaluation. But in the end, everyone seemed satisfied with the decision he made.

If the expression "Time waits for no man" is true, it especially rings true for firemen. While on duty one evening in 1973, the unit responded to a fire call on 138th Street. When they arrived, there was heavy smoke coming from the apartment building; people were running out the front door while others were using fire escapes. Cooney was the designated roof man, and as such, he went to the roof of the fire building and checked the rear of the building for fire. He also looked for anyone who might need assistance. Then he opened the roof door to relieve some of the smoke congestion on the staircase and began his descent down the staircase, floor by floor, continuing his search. The fire had already worked its way from the first to the second floor by the time he reached the third level.

As was accepted procedure for the roof man, he wore no mask, so it was necessary for him to crawl along the floor trying to avoid the heavy smoke. He crawled his way through the apartment and found a large dog dead on the floor. Then he heard a moan and located an elderly woman slumped in a chair nearby. Cooney quickly picked up the woman and, knowing the interior of the building was no longer an option, carried her out of the apartment and up to the roof. He then carried her over to the adjoining roof, where neighbors were waiting and assured him they would stay with her until an ambulance arrived. Tom was secure that she was now coherent and out of harm's way, so he returned to the fire building and continued his search. He was delighted to hear she had fully recovered after a short hospital stay, but felt badly that she had to suffer the loss of her beloved dog and her apartment.

The chief had already designated this fire a second alarm when he was made aware of Tom's actions and resulting rescue that night. When the unit returned to the firehouse, Cooney was told the chief was writing out a report on his actions that night and would be submitting it to the Board of Merit for their consideration. They reviewed the report and he was ultimately awarded a Certificate of Merit and a Service Rating: A Ribbon from the Fire Department of the City of New York, during the year 1973." Tom is a modest man who will say he is not a hero, but he was just in the right place at the right time and did what he was trained to do.

CHAPTER 15

Cooney had been a fireman for about twelve years, and his experiences working in Harlem provided him with the confidence and ability that may have been lacking in his earlier years on the job. For several of those years, his steady assignment was that of the roof man. His job was to get up to the roof as quickly as possible to vent the smoke from the interior of the building and to report back to the lieutenant the conditions in the rear of the building. In most cases the buildings were six stories or higher. The fires at the City housing projects presented additional problems because they were sixteen stories high and the elevators were usually in use or out of order. The ability to move quickly was extremely important, so it became common summer practice for the roof man to wear work boots and a denim jacket instead of the issued rubber boots and turnout coat.

The change in clothing made a ten-pound difference and gave him the extra stamina to carry the tools and complete his assignment. The chief at the scene usually made no comment about the change in a roof man's clothing because he knew the fireman was only doing it so he could get the job done faster. However, the roof man was well aware that if he was hurt at a fire and was not wearing the proper clothing, he would be held responsible. Luckily, it never became an issue for Tom, but he will admit to a few close calls.

Years later at an annual firehouse luncheon, a fellow fireman shared a memory with Cooney of the first day he met him after being assigned to the Harlem firehouse. He remembered the alarm sounded and Tom jumped on the truck wearing a helmet, denim jacket, and work boots. He was confused and surprised that no one seemed to notice that he was not in the proper turnout coat and boots. But after several more runs to the roof that same day, to six-story buildings with no elevators, he quickly came to understand why Tom chose that outfit in lieu of his turnout gear.

Firemen are a tough breed by nature, but they preserve their strength for fighting fires and keep a low profile in the neighborhood. But, at times, even firemen are not immune to the drama in the streets. One night after a fire call on 136th Street, the unit was working after the fire was out when a man came over and asked if they would move their truck so he could get his car out to go to work. The lieutenant told him it wasn't a problem and asked Cooney to please take care of it. Cooney moved the truck and was walking back to his unit when he passed a bar. Someone quite drunk came out and began shouting curse words at him. Cooney tried to ignore him and walk away, but the man started poking his finger into his chest and told him, "Your life is in my hands." Cooney told the guy to go back to the bar and stop bothering him. Suddenly there was the sound of sirens, and police came running toward the abusive man. Seeing them rushing toward him, he backed up and reached into his pocket. The police quickly jumped him and wrestled him to the ground. Then they handcuffed him, put him in the back of the squad car, and drove off without a word. A small group began to gather when they heard the sirens, and they were getting upset because they didn't know what happened. Tom went back to the unit and told his lieutenant what had transpired, and the lieutenant decided they should leave the area quickly and return to the firehouse.

They had no sooner gotten back to the firehouse when the chief called and informed them that the man Cooney had encountered on the street had been boasting to the patrons in the bar that he was going to kill a fireman. Some of the patrons who heard him say this called the police, and that's why they responded so quickly. The police also said he was bringing a gun out of his pocket, which was why they jumped him. When the rest of the firehouse heard the story, they all agreed that Tom's Badge #711 was lucky for him once again.

The police called and asked if Cooney would go downtown, with the arresting police officer, to give his account of the incident in court. He said he would, and the officer came by the firehouse the next morning to pick him up on his motorcycle. Tom reluctantly got on the back and they made their way through the heavy City traffic, downtown to the courthouse. It took the whole day for them to give their accounts of the previous night and fill out the proper paperwork. The man was indicted on the charges and plea bargained his way to just one year behind bars. When court was over, Tom took a deep breath and once again got on the motorcycle for the ride back to the firehouse. When he safely reached his destination he noted that even though this was his first ride, he was certain it would be the only ride he would ever take on a motorcycle.

Cooney's new friend in blue made it a point to stop by the firehouse to chat and enjoy a cup of coffee. Sadly, approximately six months later, the visits came to an abrupt halt. One evening while on patrol, the officer responded to a call from another local bar owner, with eerily similar circumstances to his call a few months ago. Someone in the bar was causing trouble and wielding a gun. However, this time, tragically, the officer was shot and killed during the altercation. The young officer had only been a member of the police department a few short years.

CHAPTER 16

Over the years, Tom responded to many alarms, but not all were major fires. One night they were called to a factory building that stretched a full block and was several stories high. As they pulled up to the building, they could see a bright red light glowing through all the windows. The engine company began stretching their hose lines while the ladder unit forced the front door open. As they entered the building, they realized something strange was going on: There was no smoke. They continued their search and located the building's huge coal furnace. Mystery solved. The furnace door had been left open and the coal fire inside was reflecting out through the windows of the factory. All the firemen had to do was close the furnace door and their job was done. Everyone was relieved, including the chief, who was sure when they first arrived that this would be an all-night, major fire.

On another day, Cooney was detailed to an engine company when an early morning phone alarm was called in by a policeman at the scene. The block was full of abandoned apartment buildings and there was a substantial amount of black smoke coming from a rubber-covered copper cable that had previously been used as a ground for the apartment building. They put out the fire and were ready to leave when the policeman approached the firemen and suggested they take the cable to the junkyard. He told them if they left the cable, the kids would only come back and start another fire, and they would have to come back again. So, the firemen did what the officer suggested and got enough money for the copper cable to supply the firehouse with coffee for the next year.

Being a proud dad and proud of his job, Cooney asked his lieutenant if he could bring his nine-year-old son, Edward, to work for a day during the summer vacation. He wanted to show him what life in this part of the city was like and what his father did for a living. The lieutenant said it would be okay provided he was strictly supervised. On the big day when Cooney's alarm went off at home, he woke to see Ed already dressed and ready to go. On the car ride down, Cooney explained to Ed that any time the unit responded to an alarm, he was to remain with the driver no matter what else was going on. That morning the unit was called to an oil-burner fire, and as soon as they arrived back at the firehouse, a call came in for a car fire. The owner had attempted to put the fire out himself before he rang the alarm, so the fire was fully involved when the firemen arrived. Ed watched wide-eyed as the car was reduced to burnt metal from the heat. By the time the fire was out and they returned to the firehouse, it was lunchtime.

Tom was helping with lunch when Ed came running into the kitchen to tell him there was a man out back yelling for help. He looked out the window and saw on the top floor of the adjacent building a man frantically yelling from a window filled with smoke. While he was putting on his gear, he instructed Ed to remain in the firehouse and watch from the window. The truck and engine went around the block and up to the top floor. Apparently the man had dozed off on his pile of old, thin mattresses with a lit cigarette in his mouth. Luckily he awoke when he smelled the smoke. The engine company put out the fire, then rolled up each mattress and tossed them out of the window onto the firehouse parking lot below. Cooney told his son to get a six-foot hook and together they dragged each mattress out to the front fire hydrant, where they could be totally soaked. When the rest of the firemen got back in house, they sat down to have their long-delayed lunch. At the table, they all thanked Ed for alerting them about the man in the window. Everyone agreed he did an excellent job handling the hook and the mattresses and that he would make a great fireman.

When the shift ended, father and son headed home.

When Ed's mom asked him how his day went, he said it was exciting, but quickly added that he wished his dad was anything but a fireman. He said he couldn't understand why his dad would want to run into a burning building that everyone else was trying to get out of. A year later the Cooney family grew again with the addition of another son, Kenneth, but neither one of the boys ever expressed any desire to become a fireman.

CHAPTER 17

With the birth of his second son, Kenneth, Tom's family now had five members. With a ten-year-old son, a newborn son, and a six-year-old daughter in between, Tom was giving some serious thought to converting his garage and workshop into another bedroom and a recreation room. In order to gain access to these rooms without going outside the house, Cooney would have to install a spiral staircase leading from the dining room downstairs to the floor below. He was handy, but cutting through a floor was way out of his league. So he sought the advice of a fireman, Jim, who worked in the Harlem firehouse with Tom.

Jim lived in the nearby town, and he and Tom would occasionally drive to work together when their shifts coincided. One such day, Cooney was telling his friend about his plans and without hesitation, Jim said he would be more than happy to lend a hand. The next time the two of them had some time off, Jim came over to the house, and in a few hours, they had the floor opening perfectly cut to accommodate the new spiral staircase. Jim had built his own house and was responsible for most of the renovations and conversions that were done to the kitchen and rear room at the firehouse, so Tom knew he had the right man whenever he needed advice.

One morning, returning home from a night tour, Jim had to contend with some nasty weather and heavy fog, and his car hit a boulder on the side of the road. The impact caused him to hit his head on the windshield. He continued the ride home and thought little of it. A few days later, he was at his mother's house, helping her put some boxes up in her closet, when he felt a sharp pain in his neck. He went to his doctor, who took x-rays that revealed he had broken his neck. Jim was immediately hospitalized, put in traction, and placed on medical leave while he recuperated. When his doctors told him that he was well enough to return to work, the fire department doctors told him otherwise. They said in a situations such as this, no one with that type of injury was ever put back on full duty. He then appealed their decision and had to appear before a Fire Department Medical Board. During the hearing, while he was arguing and appealing his case, he noticed that none of the doctors were even looking at the various medical reports in front of them. Getting frustrated and visibly quite upset, he told the board that the fire department was his life, and he expected them to at least read over the medical reports in front of them and review them before rendering a decision. It was an uphill battle, but in the end Jim was permitted to return to duty at the firehouse in Harlem. He continued to work at the job he loved and gave the fire department twenty-nine years of service before he finally retired.

Cooney's particular job was sometimes made more complicated by well-meaning watchdogs. Tom recalls three such stories that all ended safely and added some humorous relief, at his expense, back at the firehouse. His unit had just arrived at the scene of a two-family home, sitting in the middle of a row of two-family houses, which was on fire. His orders were to open the rear of the fire building for relief and do a search. He went through the adjoining building and was near the door when the biggest German shepherd he had ever seen came out of the shadows, jumping on him and pinning him to the wall. The dog's owner heard the barking and had to forcibly pull the dog off his chest. Cooney had to report what had happened and explain why he was unable to open the rear of the fire building as he was told to do. Needless to say he took some ribbing about it.

On another occasion the owner of the fire building had bolted the doors with several locks, so it took a little longer than usual to enter the apartment, and the smoke was building up quickly. Cooney was just about to step into the smoke-filled apartment when a large dog, in an attempt to escape the smoke, came charging out and knocked him to the ground, Back at the firehouse, they all joked about it, as Tom told them it took him a few seconds to figure out what hit him.

The third incident happened after the fire had been successfully extinguished. The firemen were still overhauling and gathering their equipment from the two apartments involved in the fire. Cooney had removed his heavy turnout coat and put it aside on the floor while he took another quick look around the two apartments. Suddenly a big boxer appeared that was obviously in an agitated state—jumping, snarling, and barking. He apparently had found himself a hiding spot during the fire, but was still feeling the effects of the smoke and was not happy at seeing the intruding firemen. The men were able to contain the dog in one of the two rooms. Unfortunately, it was the same room where Tom had left his turnout coat. So he took his six-foot hook and while another fireman distracted the dog, he managed to pull his coat to safety. The firemen were pleased to learn the boxer had fully recovered and was back to his duties as watchdog by the time they left.

CHAPTER 18

An alarm that Cooney will never forget began in the early morning hours at the end of a night tour, on Sunday, August 25, 1974. When Ladder Co. 30 arrived at the scene, some civilians quickly alerted the captain of a woman screaming for help and threatening to jump from her fifth-floor window. The fire was in full force in the apartment below hers, forcing her to retreat to the shaft window as her last possible spot of refuge. Her desperation was understandable, as the tremendous amount of smoke billowing out from the apartment below had nearly rendered her obscured from view. Any attempt to reach and rescue her by fire escape was now no longer an option. She was trapped and obviously in a full state of panic, having no means of escape.

The captain told the chauffeur to drive the front wheels of the truck onto the sidewalk at an angle that would allow the 100-foot rear mount ladder to secure the best advantage to reach the window in hopes of providing a slim chance for a rescue. The chauffeur succeeded in placing the nearly fully extended aerial in the shaft and up against the window edge, just as flames blew out the window from the apartment below. Cooney then, according to part of The Report of Meritorious Act, "without regard for his own safety and without hesitation, quickly ascended the ladder and reaching the flame exposure, he pressed himself to the left side of the aerial and pushed past the flames and heat." Tom continued his climb and reached the distraught woman, but now was confronted by the problem of getting her out of the window and onto the aerial. The woman was tall and heavyset in stature, and the window was a mere 16" X 36" in size. To add to the difficulty, the window was covered by a storm window, and the ladder was resting against it, so the sash could not be raised. Cooney told the woman to turn her head and shield her face as he proceeded to break the glass and rip out the aluminum frame, which landed over the top of the ladder. His adrenaline pumping, he reached in and grabbed the woman, and despite her size, he was able to pull her up and out through the small window, across the sill, over the aluminum frame, and onto the extended ladder. At this point they were enveloped by smoke, and the heat became more intense. By keeping the woman on the left side of the ladder, Cooney managed to shield her with his body while passing the erupting fire on the fourth floor. They continued their descent slowly down the ladder, and when the smoke began to clear, they were greeted by cheers from the waiting neighbors on the sidewalk below. The woman was treated for smoke inhalation and cuts to her right leg and transported to St. Luke's hospital for further treatment, where she made a full recovery.

Cooney truly saved her life and was praised for his actions. He received his second Certificate of Merit and Service Rating, and a ribbon from the Fire Department of the City of New York.

Fire at 319 W 124th ST NYC

CHAPTER 19
THE BUCKLEY YEARS

Financially speaking, with a wife, three growing children, and a mortgage, Cooney was always willing to work extra hours to supplement the family income. So, throughout the years he found several different part-time jobs to keep him busy. He started with a short-lived window-washing business in Queens, which he had to give up when transferred to different firehouse locations. He was a house painter, an auto-parts delivery man, and a UPS delivery man during the holidays. All these efforts, however, were not permanent and Cooney needed something steady and more reliable. As fate would have it, in the spring of 1973, he was offered such a job.

A fireman in his unit, named Gerry Garvey asked Tom if he might be interested in a part-time chauffeur job. Cooney was an experienced driver but had never given much thought to chauffeuring; he said he would be willing to give it a try. It turned out to be one of the best decisions he would ever make. The person his buddy was driving needed someone to take him to and from numerous important functions throughout the entire week. Gerry said he could not handle it all without it seriously affecting his main job as a firefighter. He then went on to say that he had already spoken to his employer, who had no problem with splitting the hours in the week with a second man, as long as he had someone available to him all week.

And so it was that Cooney was introduced to and became acquainted with William F. Buckley, Jr., who was, among other things, editor of the *National Review* magazine, a syndicated columnist, author of several books, and the host of a television show entitled *Firing Line*. He was also a noted lecturer and a delegate to the United Nations. Tom was to be Mr. Buckley's driver for part of the week, and the rest of the week keep up with his main job with the fire department.

Tom and Mr. Buckley hit it off well from the start, and they shared a happy working friendship for many years. Today, in remembering his late friend, Cooney says, "Mr. Buckley was a good person and a real gentleman. I was only able to handle the long hours and busy schedules of the two jobs because he and Mrs. Buckley were always so pleasant and considerate, and that added enjoyment to the job."

Cooney's partner, Gerry, lived on the outskirts of the city, while Tom resided with his family much further north in the suburbs. Mr. Buckley was aware of this, so when he knew Tom had no night shift scheduled at the firehouse, he would have Tom pick him up in the morning as usual and try to send him home early, so he could have a few extra hours with his family. He told Tom not to worry, he would simply take a taxi back home at the end of the day. And whenever Mr. Buckley would go on one of his many circuit lecturing trips, at each stop he would first look for the person in charge and ask them to "please take good care of my driver." He would also do this when he appeared on the many television shows as a guest speaker.

Mr. Buckley was well known for his expertise on the subject of fine wine. He lived in a two-story Manhattan townhouse on the East 70's, which included a basement that housed two wine vaults. Cooney remembers one particular evening, driving Mr. and Mrs. Buckley to a hotel on Fifth Avenue, where he was attending an elaborate fund-raiser dinner hosted by the Conservative Party. For the event he donated twelve cases of a special French wine, which he had delivered to the hotel earlier in the week Tom had dropped them off at the hotel and was heading home when he received an unexpected call on the car phone. It was Mr. Buckley asking him to please go back to the apartment to get twelve more cases of the French wine and deliver them to the hotel, as quickly as possible. Apparently, when the first cases arrived at the hotel, they were left standing up by a misguided young waiter, instead of being placed on their side. The error in the misplacement of the bottles somehow adversely affected the taste of the wine. While Mr. Buckley was not pleased about the loss of twelve cases of fine wine, he was happy that he could rectify the situation in time for the dinner to be a big success.

On his next night tour at the firehouse, Cooney's unit responded to a building with a fire in progress in the first-floor apartment. His job was to search the floor above. Cooney climbed the fire escape and entered a window on the second floor. When he stepped inside the room, he began to bump into, trip over, and fall against miscellaneous boxes, piled as high as the ceiling. Due to the heavy smoke, visibility was very poor, but somehow he managed to check out the rest of the apartment, taking quite a beating along the way. As the fire below was starting to come under control, the smoke on the second floor started to clear. Cooney was then better able to check out his surroundings. It appeared as if the apartment was being used as a storage place for stolen merchandise. The apartment was filled with boxes and bins containing TVs, washers, dryers, and assorted furniture pieces. Cooney reported what he had found to his lieutenant, who in turn notified the police. When he returned to the firehouse all bruised, he took a deep breath and joked that he felt like he had been hit by a truck.

CHAPTER 20

Being a chauffeur can lead to many different kinds of assignments, and driving for someone like Mr. Buckley was always interesting. One such day, Cooney picked up Mr. Buckley and his television producer from Kennedy Airport, who were coming back from a combination vacation/business trip in Switzerland. Cooney drove Mr. Buckley home first and had just dropped off his producer friend at his home when the car phone rang. Mr. Buckley was missing his briefcase and was wondering if he had left it in the backseat of the car. Tom checked and said it was not there. After checking to make sure the producer had not inadvertently picked it up, Mr. Buckley asked Tom if he would return to Kennedy Airport to see if he could locate the briefcase, which he remembered having when he left the plane. By the time Tom got back to the airport, Mr.

Buckley had already called ahead and informed them of the lost briefcase. Tom looked everywhere he thought Mr. Buckley could have left it and spoke with personnel throughout the airport, all to no avail. He was just about to give up when he spotted a small baggage room on a side wall. He inquired about it and learned it was luggage that was being returned to Europe. He sought an employee, explained his dilemma, and asked if he might search the room briefly. It took awhile, but Tom located the briefcase, with a tag on it directing it back to Switzerland. Tom tipped the employee, thanking him for his help in locating the briefcase in time, and rushed to call Mr. Buckley with the good news.

When he returned to the Manhattan apartment with the briefcase, Mr. Buckley was waiting for him with sandwiches and coffee. He sat down with Tom and told him the reason he was so anxious to find his briefcase was because it contained all the notes and drafts he had just completed for his new book. He was relieved and happy that the briefcase was found and, patting Tom on the shoulder, thanked him again. The book, *United Nations Journal: A Delegate's Odyssey*, was subsequently published in 1974, and when it was released, Mr. Buckley gave Tom an autographed copy "to help you remember the part you played in getting it written."

Mr. Buckley was known for his love of the sea and especially enjoyed sailing. He owned a spacious yacht named *Cyrano*, which, due to its eighty-foot length, required a licensed captain to operate. Unfortunately, Mr. Buckley's busy schedule kept him from using it very often, so his accountant suggested that it might be more practical to consider leasing the craft out for charter usage rather than letting it sit idle, waiting to be used. Mr. Buckley hesitated but then reluctantly agreed, and the first two charters went well. The third time around, the boat was chartered by a company who wanted to treat some employees to an evening cruise around Manhattan Island. As the craft made its way down the Hudson River and under the George Washington Bridge, one of the passengers leaning against a rope rail fell overboard and into the murky water. Every attempt was made to rescue him, but the strong current swiftly pulled him under to his death. His body was not recovered until the following day. The case went to court, but neither the boat nor the boat's captain were ever found to be at fault. The incident was declared a tragic accident.

Mr. Buckley was upset over the news of the accident, so when his accountant suggested he sell half of his share of the boat and split the cost of upkeep with a partner, he agreed. One day Cooney drove Mr. Buckley to the airport to pick up a prospective buyer and take him up to his house in Stamford for the weekend to check out the yacht and possibly negotiate a sale. On the way to Stamford, the gentleman told Mr. Buckley that he was actually a pilot, not a sailor, and when he returned home to Alaska at the end of World War II, he began a business flying people to hunting camps. One day, a man who identified himself as "a government employee" approached him and said that the U.S. government wanted to get beef livestock to places not accessible by either land or sea. This prospective yachtsman said that the only solution would be to have the cows parachuted into these areas. The government liked the idea, and when he gave it a try, it proved to be successful. The gentleman went on to say he made enough money from this venture to start his own airline, which he called Alaska Airlines. Mr. Buckley later told Tom it was an interesting meeting, but in the end they could not reach an agreement on the terms of sharing the yacht, so the deal could not be completed.

A big smile comes across Cooney's face when he talks about Mr. and Mrs. Buckley's family dog, a King Charles cavalier cocker spaniel named Rollie. The dog was a family favorite and very often accompanied Mr. Buckley in the backseat of the limo as he shuttled between meetings and appointments. Of course while he was at these meetings, Rollie also spent a great deal of time with Gerry and Tom and became quite attached to them. This affection and loyalty to Tom inadvertently led to a quick television appearance for the two of them.

One morning Cooney picked up Mr. Buckley and Rollie for a ride to Philadelphia for an appearance on the *Mike Douglas* show. When they arrived, Mr. Buckley asked Cooney to bring Rollie upstairs into the studio with him. As Mr. Buckley was preparing to go on stage, Tom and Rollie got to meet some of the other guests of the day, including Tricia Nixon, the president's daughter, and the famed singer Robert Goulet. Miss Nixon immediately fell in love with Rollie, while Robert Goulet took an instant liking to Cooney and they began to chat. By now, Mr. Buckley was in the studio with Mike Douglas, and somehow their talk turned to dogs. Mr. Buckley told his host that he had his faithful companion, Rollie, with him, and Mr. Douglas asked his guest to bring the dog out on stage. Mr. Buckley called to the dog, and Rollie, hearing his owner's voice, headed toward the stage. Suddenly he stopped and looked at Tom, then back to his owner, not quite sure what to do. Tom encouraged him to go, but still the dog hesitated, not wanting to leave him. Mr. Buckley called him again, but Rollie stood his ground. So Tom quickly put Rollie on his leash and escorted him onstage. He handed him over to Mr. Buckley, then went back off-camera but stayed near the curtain so Rollie could still see him. On the way home, Mr. Buckley made several comments about the dog's torn loyalty, but told Tom he was not offended. He told Rollie he still loved him and seemed quite amused by the whole incident.

CHAPTER 21

As a United Nations delegate under President Richard M. Nixon, Mr. Buckley would travel to the Pentagon in Washington, DC for monthly meetings. One night, Cooney was waiting at LaGuardia Airport for Mr. Buckley's 6 p.m. shuttle to return from Washington, but when the flight landed, Mr. Buckley was not on it. Cooney then contacted Mr. Buckley's secretary, who said she had not heard from him, but he may have missed the flight. She asked him to please wait for the next flight. Tom waited for the 7 p.m., 8 p.m., and 9 p.m. shuttles, while keeping in contact with Mr. Buckley's secretary, who in turn was still trying to contact Mr. Buckley. No one else had heard from him either. Tom continued to wait, growing more apprehensive as each hourly shuttle arrived without his boss on it. He thought possibly a new crisis had developed somewhere that he was not aware of, and the Pentagon meeting was still in session. Or he hoped that because it was so late, his boss had decided to stay overnight and forgot to call. Just then the last midnight shuttle from Washington, DC landed and Mr. Buckley stepped off the plane. When he got into the car, Mr. Buckley told Cooney he would not believe what he was about to hear.

He then went on to tell the story of how he was the last one to leave the Pentagon meeting room. He got on the elevator to the garage to meet up with his driver for the ride to the airport. When he reached the garage level, he got out of the elevator, walked to the exit sign, and waited for the security man to buzz the exit door open. And that's when things started to go very wrong. He waited patiently, but when there was no response, he began to bang on the door and yell, trying to garner someone's attention, but all to no avail. He said he went back to the elevator, because the same security man who controlled the door should have been keeping an eye on the security monitor cameras as well. But that brought no response or results either. Nor did several more desperate attempts to attract attention. Then finally, after being stuck in the corridor for several hours, someone did notice him and buzzed the exit door open. Mr. Buckley then found someone who made a few frantic phone calls on his behalf, resulting in a police escort to the airport, just in time to make the last flight back to New York. On the ride home from the airport, Mr. Buckley picked up the car phone and called Vice President Agnew to inform him about the incident and to tell him what he thought about the Pentagon's security. Cooney can only guess what became of the security guard on duty that night, but speculates that it didn't end well for him.

One of Mr. Buckley's closest friends was the celebrity and motion-picture actor David Niven. One evening Cooney was asked to pick up Mr. Niven from his hotel and drive him up to the Buckleys' Stamford, Connecticut, house for the weekend. The traveling Englishman was in this country for a lecture tour, to talk about his first published book, *The Moon's a Balloon*. Knowing his wife, Edie, was a big fan of Mr. Niven's, Cooney purchased a copy before the trip, and on the ride up to Stamford, he asked Mr. Niven if he might autograph the book for her. Mr. Niven said he would be happy to do so. As they continued to chat, Tom told Mr. Niven that his wife had tried to get a ticket to his book signing and lecture, which was being held at a restaurant in the next town from where they lived, but none were available at any price. Smiling, Mr. Niven autographed the book, writing, "For Edie, Sorry to miss you at Perona Farms. You won't miss anything, I promise! Very Sincerely, David Niven." He jokingly told Tom to thank his wife for purchasing his book, since she made him seventeen cents richer. The book was a hit and went on to become number one on the *New York Times* best seller list.

A few days later, while driving back down from Stamford, Mr. Niven asked Tom if he would mind making a stop before he dropped him off at his Manhattan hotel. Tom drove him to the store he requested, and Mr. Niven hurried out of the limo, into the store, and returned with his purchase a few minutes later. When they arrived at the hotel, Mr. Niven told Tom how much he enjoyed his company on the ride back, and as he got out of the limo, he handed Tom the purchase he had just made at the store: "When you get home, have a drink on me."

Mr. and Mrs. Buckley owned a chalet in Switzerland, and every year they would plan a combined business and pleasure trip from January to March. While they were there, Mr. Buckley would take business trips throughout Europe to conduct interviews and meet with notable personalities for his television program, *Firing Line*, while Mrs. Buckley enjoyed spending the time with friends and hosting dinner parties. Cooney recalls the year they came back from Switzerland much earlier than expected, and Mr. Buckley related why their trip was cut short. He told Tom they were hosting a small dinner party for friends, and David Niven was one of the invited guests. When Mr. Niven arrived, he thought he noticed smoke coming from the top of the roof and began banging loudly on the front door. When a startled Mr. Buckley answered the door,

Mr. Niven asked him, in typical British demeanor, if he was aware that his roof was smoking and on fire! Fortunately, everyone had enough time to get out of the house safely. Unfortunately, the chalet was located in such a remote area, the firemen could not reach it in time to save any part of it. It burned to the ground.

Working a second job is never easy, but it has its perks when your employers are as pleasant and considerate as Mr. Buckley and Mrs. Buckley. One day Cooney was waiting for Mr. Buckley in front of the National Review office when he surprised him and came out earlier than usual and seemed in a hurry to get home. He told Cooney he was running late for a formal luncheon that Mrs. Buckley was hosting, and the guest of honor was Governor Ronald Regan of California. When they arrived at the apartment, Mr. Buckley suggested that since it was hot out, Tom should come inside and have some lunch. He also asked him to take care of the governor's two California police escorts, who were sitting out front in the car. When Tom found out they had not eaten yet, he invited them to come inside to the kitchen to meet Maria, the family's longtime cook. Maria sat them down, but instead of giving them a sandwich, as Tom expected, she served them the same meal that the governor and the rest of the guests were enjoying in the main dining room. After the meal, the surprised and now well-fed police escorts returned to their car, but not before they gave Tom an addresses and telephone numbers where they could be reached in case he ever came out to California. They said they were taken aback by his kind gesture, since they were usually left to fend for themselves on the cross-country stops, and they were so appreciative, they hoped they could return the favor someday.

Cooney has many memories of the Buckleys' generous spirit, particularly around Christmas. Many a night they would take a cab back from a social event just so Gerry or Tom could get home early to spend extra time with their respective families during the holidays. Mr. Buckley would give the partners a bonus to share with their families, and Mrs. Buckley would go out and shop for something special and personal for each of them.

CHAPTER 22

Firemen may come in all sizes, but the ones in the Harlem firehouse all had a big heart. Cooney notes that his firehouse was one of the first to start an annual Christmas party for the neighborhood children. They would ask one of the African-American firemen to dress up as Santa Claus, and on the day of the party, he would ride around the block on top of the ladder truck. He would call out to the children to come to the firehouse for cookies and milk; then the rest of the men would hand out gifts as well. One year, the fire commissioner heard about the party and asked to be invited. So, they invited him, and when he came, so did the press. The commissioner was mingling and cordially greeting people when he was introduced to a successful businessman from the area. The press took their picture, but, much to the commissioner's dismay, he later learned that this businessman was really the local "numbers man." Not exactly the kind of person a fire commissioner would want to be seen talking with, let alone be photographed together. He was further displeased the next morning when the photo made the front page of one of the City's daily newspapers. Cooney notes that due to the incident, it took the Harlem firehouse a long time to get back in the commissioner's good graces.

One afternoon, Tom found himself with some extra time on his hands, as Mr. Buckley was busy in the office for the day. Since he was scheduled to be at the firehouse for the night shift and was the designated cook, he decided to pick up something for supper from the butcher shop on 86th Street. He wanted to get something different for a change and decided he would make his family's favorite German sauerbraten meal. Along with the meat, the butcher included the pickled juice necessary for marinating the meat and making the gravy. However, the pickled juice had a strong odor to it before it was cooked, so Tom decided to put the meat and juice in the trunk of the limo before picking up his boss for the ride home. Soon after getting into the car, Mr. Buckley asked about the smell and wondered if anything was wrong with the car. Cooney assured him the car was fine. When they arrived at the townhouse, he asked about the odor again. By now Tom felt he owed him an explanation and told him about the dinner and the cause of the odor. Mr. Buckley laughed and told Tom if he didn't have guests coming for dinner that evening, he would have loved to join him and his firemen friends at the firehouse instead.

On another day, Tom was Mr. Buckley's driver for the day, but had to be at the firehouse for the 6 p.m.-9 a.m. shift that night. Mr. Buckley needed to return to Stamford that evening, so Tom asked if it would be okay if he drove him as far as the Harlem firehouse and stopped to change drivers. His partner, Gerry, would be coming off the 9 a.m.-6 p.m. day shift and could then take him up the rest of the way. From time to time, Mr. Buckley would ask Tom and Gerry about their fireman jobs and was curious to see where his drivers worked, so he was quick to say he had no problem with the plan. The nearer they came to the firehouse, the more the neighborhood scenery changed and the less inclined Mr. Buckley became to leave the confines of his car. However, when the limo pulled up in front of the firehouse, all the firemen came out to meet "the celebrity," and Mr. Buckley cordially returned the greetings while Tom and Gerry quickly changed uniforms and made the switch.

Friday morning started out routine with Cooney picking up his boss at his apartment and driving him to his office. The ride took about fifteen minutes, and in that short time, Mr. Buckley would write his syndicated column for the daily newspapers. Tom ran some errands and was asked to be back by 3 p.m. to pick him up because he was to be the guest speaker at the

University of Pennsylvania that evening. It was 5 p.m. before Mr. Buckley came down from his office and they could set off on their interstate trip. By now it was rush hour and the trip across town and through the Lincoln Tunnel was slow going. Once they got onto the highway, Tom upped the pace considerably and they made it to the university on time. Grateful that Tom got him there in time and always mindful of him, Mr. Buckley once again sought out the man in charge and made sure he would take care of his driver. This was a common practice, and not until he was satisfied it would be taken care of would Mr. Buckley go in to join his host. So, Tom spent the evening listening to his boss speak while sitting at his own table, having a four-course dinner.

Later, as they were driving home, Mr. Buckley wanted to know if he might drive for a while to give Tom a rest, but Tom declined the offer. They made their way up to the weekend house in Stamford and finally arrived there at 3 a.m. Mr. Buckley asked Tom to stay the night and wait till morning to make the trip home. Tom thanked him, but had to decline the offer in order to get home to fulfill his promise to his son, Ken, to take him on a Cub Scout hike scheduled early Saturday morning. It took some three more hours of driving to get home, and that gave him just enough time to change clothes and grab a roll and coffee. Tom and Ken went on the hike and even managed to have a good time. But when they got home late Saturday

CHAPTER 22

afternoon, Tom bid everyone a good night and went straight to bed. He slept the rest of Saturday and most of the day Sunday. He had truly earned that long, uninterrupted sleep and needed it before his busy week began again.

There were always some light moments during the work week, and one of Cooney's favorite stories deals with his chauffeur partner. Gerry, who was a huge NY Giants fan, had season tickets to their home games. His Saturday routine, when he was the scheduled driver, would be to pick up Mrs. Buckley at her Manhattan apartment. They would then make a few stops at the local shops before embarking on the drive to their weekend retreat in Stamford. Once they arrived, Gerry would bring in all the packages and hurry to help Mrs. Buckley unpack and settle in so he could leave, with the hope that he would make the Giants game in time. However, Mrs. Buckley would be concerned that Gerry had such an early and busy morning, and she would not let him leave until he had some lunch. She would then insist that Gerry sit down at the kitchen table while she proceeded to prepare him a nice big sandwich and then served him. Gerry would chew and swallow the sandwich as quickly as possible, politely thank Mrs. Buckley for lunch, and rush back to the City as fast as he could to get to the game. He never had the heart to tell her that due to her kind gesture, he missed all the opening plays at most of the Giants games.

Cooney found himself with a couple of hours off between taking Mr. Buckley to appointments and decided to visit Gerry at the firehouse to discuss next week's schedule. Tom, as usual, had the family dog, Rollie, with him, and the firemen were busy playing with him when suddenly an alarm came in. All three companies were responding, and as Gerry got to the truck and began climbing up to the tiller seat, Rollie responded too, by running right after Gerry and the truck. Cooney was feverishly trying to catch the dog to stop him from chasing the truck, which had already come as close as it could get without hitting him. Fortunately, he was able to grab him and get a leash on him before he made another sudden move. Tom was visibly shaken and upset the rest of the day just thinking of what might have happened, and he vowed he would make sure not to let any situation like this ever present itself again.

CHAPTER 23

Cooney's job as a chauffeur between firehouse shifts provided interesting intervals, but being a fireman first and foremost always brought him back to reality. He recalls the time they discovered the body of a woman during a final search, in another part of the building, after the apartment fire had been extinguished. Her death appeared suspicious and the police were called in to investigate. They asked the firemen if they could borrow their body bag for the woman while they waited for someone from the coroner's office to arrive. When the men from the coroner's office left, they inadvertently took the fire unit's body bag instead of transferring the woman into one of their own. About a week later, remembering Cooney was in the downtown area when he worked his side job, his firehouse called, asking him to go to the morgue and pick up their bag. When he arrived at the morgue, he only had to show his badge and was directed down to the basement. Where he had to pass the area where they were performing autopsies, he was asked the woman's name, which Cooney truthfully admitted he did not know. What followed was a search through twenty individual lockers until they found the right woman. Cooney still shudders when he thinks about that scene and remembers hoping he would never have to visit that downtown building again.

When you work for an active and world-renowned family like the Buckleys, you never know where you might be going or whom you are likely to meet. One morning Cooney picked up Mr. and Mrs. Buckley at their townhouse and soon he was on his way to Boston, where Mr. Buckley had a speaking engagement. When they arrived, Mr. Buckley told him he had the night off and what time he was needed the next morning. Tom remembers driving around Boston, taking in the sights, when he spotted a firehouse. He says, "I stopped in, told them I was a NYC fireman, and was wondering if they could recommend a reasonable hotel for me to stay at for the night. They told me I didn't need any recommendations, because I would be staying at the firehouse with them." Tom agreed, but insisted on treating the firemen to dinner. They talked quite a bit during dinner, and when they found out where Cooney worked, he was surprised to learn they were familiar with the area. It seemed they had been to New York City several times to play softball against other fire units in Harlem.

The following morning, Tom was waiting in front of the hotel for Mr. and Mrs. Buckley when someone suddenly opened the back door and entered the limo. Cooney, a bit baffled, looked into the rearview mirror and was surprised to see that the towering gentleman looking back at him was none other than the famed movie star of *Ben Hur*, Mr. Charlton Heston. Tom quickly explained who he was and that he was waiting for Mr. and Mrs. Buckley. Mr. Heston laughed and apologized, saying he thought this was his ride. As he exited the car, he told Tom, "Say hello to Mr. Buckley for me and tell him I'm sorry I had to miss him."

Being a husband, parent, fireman, and homeowner, Tom found there were always adjustments that had to be made along the way. But one day he was made acutely aware that his adjustments were just minor and not a way of life. Cooney remembers standing outside the firehouse talking with another fireman when a neighbor from the block returned from a store with two large packages. One of the bags began to tear, and Cooney assisted the woman by carrying the torn bag to the front of her building. The next day she came back to thank him with a homemade pie and stayed to chat with the firemen. They began to talk about the hot weather, and she mentioned she was looking forward to going away for a few days to the country the following week. She went on to say that her husband and daughter were away this week, and next week would be her turn. The fireman, kidding with her, said, "Separate vacations might not be such a bad idea." The woman smiled and agreed with him, but said in her case it was not by choice. She explained further that one of them had to stay in the apartment at all times for fear someone might break in and take everything, and there would be nothing left when they returned. Tom couldn't help but think what a sad way it was to have to live your life.

Some days as a driver were routine and others definitely were not. A prime example was the day Mr. Buckley asked Cooney to do him a favor and come into the City on his day off. He said he was conducting an interview with a man named Edgar Smith, who had just been released from prison after thirty-two years and was still very much in the public eye. Smith, who had been convicted and sentenced to death for the murder of a fifteen-year-old girl, continued to maintain his innocence and spent his prison time trying to obtain an appeal, which were all repeatedly dismissed. In 1962, knowing Mr. Buckley was a "law and order conservative," he started sending him letters with details of his appeals. By 1965, at the insistence of someone he knew very well, Mr. Buckley consented to review the transcripts and began to have some doubts of his own about Smith's guilt. Mr. Buckley made a comment to that effect during a magazine interview, and it drew national media attention. By 1971, Edgar Smith's nineteenth appeal won him a repeat trial, provided he would accept a charge of second-degree murder, which he did. The judge granted him a pardon and he was released the next day.

Mr. Buckley, knowing the press would be out in full force, asked Tom to be at the West 54th Street TV studio before the scheduled interview. When he got to the studio, it was already packed with reporters. So, Tom called on the car phone and asked his boss to come to the freight elevator, knock on the door, and he would then help him reach the studio and avoid the press. When they arrived, Tom's partner, Gerry, got out of the car and went to the elevator door, but the press spotted him and all came running out of the studio and into the freight elevator. As Tom was trying to close the elevator door, the reporters were taking his picture and asking him how it felt to be out of prison and did he really kill the girl? He tried to convince them he was not Smith and finally had to show them his driver's license to prove it. Meanwhile, seeing the press run into the elevator, Mr. Buckley and Smith walked unnoticed into the studio. The reporters were not pleased that they had been fooled again.

A few years later, while living in California, Smith kidnapped a young lady and threatened to kill her, but fortunately the victim managed to get away. Smith was desperately seeking help and called Mr. Buckley, who refused to have anything to do with him. He called the FBI instead, and Smith ended up back in prison. Mr. Buckley later wrote a column about how deeply he regretted that he had ever been involved with Smith in the first place.

CHAPTER 24

One morning in January 1977, Mr. Buckley told Cooney they would be taking a trip up to the Catskills in New York State to check out an old abandoned freight rail line that Mr. Buckley was interested in pursuing. Mr. Buckley's attorney and a reporter went along for the ride. The reporter was invited to visit the rail line in order to write an article about its possible potential to pique any interest from tourists and skiers in the metropolitan area. When they reached the rail line station, Mr. Buckley had arranged to have them all taken by a rail car the rest of the way, to the end of the line. Unfortunately, the track had not been used for a long time, and the overgrowth of brush and small trees made this trek very difficult and time consuming. Tom, meanwhile, was sent ahead and asked to find an open spot to meet the group about half-way through the trip. After several challenging hours, the group arrived and there was Cooney, all set up with a table and chairs and ready for lunch. The reporter was amazed, noting that only Mr. Buckley could pull off a lunch in the middle of nowhere. The group finished eating and finished the trip to the end of the line, where Tom was again waiting.

On the long ride back to Manhattan, they would be passing near Tom's residence, so he asked Mr. Buckley if he would like to stop at his house for a few minutes to stretch a bit and meet his wife, Edie. He said sure, and so Mrs. Cooney finally got to meet the charming Mr. Buckley. The newspaper story, however, didn't seem to generate much interest, and so Mr. Buckley decided to forget about the project.

Thomas Cooney - Edith Cooney - W.F. Buckley - Donald Peusner

CHAPTER 24

Cooney has many fond memories of his years as a part-time chauffeur. One particular enjoyable memory was the evening he drove Mrs. Buckley and some friends to the theater. She asked Tom to stop at the Waldorf-Astoria hotel to pick up another friend who would be joining them. That friend turned out to be a favorite of Tom's, Mr. Bing Crosby. When they arrived at the theater and Mr. Crosby stepped out of the car, he looked weathered by his years and seemed to be in poor health. Nevertheless, his demeanor remained as charming as ever. As Tom closed the door behind Mr. Crosby, he touched his arm and hastily said he wanted to thank him on behalf of his mother, for the many years of pleasure his music had given to her, and that he, too, was a big fan. With that he thanked Tom, tipped his hat, and smiled that familiar Crosby smile. It was a moment to remember. Sadly, Mr. Crosby passed away a few short months later.

Cooney was working his second night tour of the week and was scheduled to pick up Mr. Buckley at his townhouse at ten the following morning. Around 5 a.m. his company responded to a two-alarm fire, which took considerable time to fully extinguish. The smoke condition in the fire building was particularly intense, so the chief told the company lieutenant that he wanted him to take all his men to the hospital to be checked out. It soon became apparent that Tom would be unable to pick up Mr. Buckley on time. When he called

Mr. Buckley, he said not to worry; he would get himself to the office and meet up with him later. That evening when Tom dropped Mr. Buckley off at his apartment, he was invited in for a cup of tea. Mr. Buckley surprised him by asking if he had ever considered leaving the Harlem firehouse and working some other job in the fire department. He went on to say that he and Mrs. Buckley were concerned about his many close calls and that he and Gerry were working in such a busy firehouse. They talked for a while and Tom said he would give it some thought. The next day, he had a long talk with his partner, Gerry, and they both agreed that it might be time for them to consider a change. They called Mr. Buckley, who was happy to hear the news and told them he would get back to them. No more than a week later, Mr. Buckley told Tom that a friend of his was soon to become the next first deputy fire commissioner and that he had highly recommended them if the commissioner needed someone to fill a driving position.

CHAPTER 25

Cooney admits he was apprehensive on the way to his first meeting with the new first deputy fire commissioner. However, right from the very first handshake, all went well and he was totally relaxed. The commissioner told Tom he already knew everything about him, and looked forward to meeting him and working together. He then told Cooney a little about himself. He said he was a battalion chief who had been in charge of the Division of Fire Prevention before his retirement. He was working for the Hilton Hotel chain as a fire consultant when the present fire commissioner asked him to come back to the fire department as his first deputy assistant. The fire commissioner asked his new first deputy to go to all major alarms and then report back on the performance of the fire units at the scene

The first Deputy told the Commissioner

Whenever he was called to a major fire, his only concern was to see that any firemen who were hurt received the best treatment possible. He also noted that the chiefs in charge at the scene were more than capable of putting out the fires with or without his help. Cooney knew right then that he was going to like working for the new first deputy.

Tom understood that as a driver for the new deputy, his role would be that of a non-firefighting nature, and that took a little getting used to. On the plus side, he realized that he would probably be getting home earlier in the evenings since this would likely be more of a daytime job. Tom and Gerry were also given the option of scheduling and switching their work days during the week between the fire department and driving Mr. Buckley, or simply working an entire week for the fire department and then an entire week with Mr. Buckley. It was decided it would cause less confusion and be easier to keep track of who was where and when if they worked a full week at a time. Tom was delighted that the new working arrangements proved to be more favorable to him and his family.

The first deputy quickly realized that Tom and Gerry were not only good drivers, but very capable of handling most any situation. He was concerned some of the other chiefs in the surrounding offices at headquarters would most certainly ask to borrow Tom for some pet projects of their own. To avoid this, he told Tom and Gerry to drop him off at the office and wait downstairs near the car radio, and he would call when he needed them. So, they soon became known as the "phantom aides" because they could rarely be found.

The new first deputy made it clear that he would employ an open-door policy among the firemen and be willing to discuss any problem or serious concern they might have. Word spread quickly and it did not take long before there was someone in his office every day.

It was also his job as first deputy commissioner to be a representative for the fire department at various dinners and functions around the City. One night Cooney dropped him and his wife off at the prestigious Downtown Athletic Club and was told to meet his boss upstairs. Tom parked the car and went into the club, where he happened to meet another fireman, and together they headed up to the eighth floor. When they got there, a waiter met them and led them to an empty dinner table. Tom began to look around for his boss and his wife, but they were nowhere to be found. He continued his search until he finally found them at a different dinner party on the floor above. Tom explained he was told the wrong floor number, and they said to stay where he was and enjoy his meal with his new fireman friend. He went back downstairs and joined the fireman for dinner and then found out he was actually at the Annual Heisman Trophy Awards dinner. Later when Tom met up with his boss in the lobby, the deputy's wife asked him how he enjoyed his meal. Tom replied that it was the best prime rib dinner he'd had in a very long time. They began to laugh and told him he was lucky; they were served corned beef and cabbage at their dinner party.

Over the next four years, Cooney and the first deputy responded to many major fires. Unfortunately some ended tragically, and out of respect and because the deputy and Tom were still firemen, they went to many funerals as well. One incident that Tom recalls as being particularly difficult happened sometime in August of 1976, as they were leaving the office for the day. A radio call came in announcing a serious factory fire and "possible loss of life." A young, newly promoted lieutenant had been assigned to an engine company and was on his very first night shift when an alarm sounded and his unit responded to a factory fire in the Ridgewood section of Queens. When they arrived, as was the lieutenant's job, he entered the building first to pinpoint the location of the fire, in order to direct his men and the hose lines accordingly. As he entered the building, suddenly and with no prior warning, some machinery came crashing down from the floor above. The machinery broke through the first floor, straight into the basement, sweeping the lieutenant along with it. Rescue attempts to reach the trapped lieutenant began immediately. However, when they reached him, they were unable to revive him as he had already succumbed to his injuries.

Tom and the commissioner arrived as the fire

CHAPTER 25

department chaplain and engine company firemen were carrying the lieutenant's body out of the building and into the ambulance. The first deputy asked Tom to drive the chaplain to the lieutenant's home to break the news to the family. When they arrived at the house, the chaplain asked Tom to accompany him inside, stating he could use his support. Tom looked surprised, and the priest said, "Even for me it never gets any easier to deliver the devastating news to a young wife and mother that she just became a widow."

Two years later, in August 1978, Cooney was just picking up the first deputy for the day when he got the call to respond to a major alarm in the Sheepshead Bay section of Brooklyn. It was at the Waldbaum Supermarket, which was presently undergoing renovations. Smoke was spotted coming from the mezzanine area and quickly spread throughout the store. It became a second-alarm fire within minutes. While the engine companies were busy with hose lines downstairs, twenty-four firemen climbed up to the roof to ventilate the blazing cock loft. Suddenly the roof collapsed, sending twelve firemen into the inferno below. Rescue operations began immediately, but access to the trapped firemen proved difficult. It was recorded that it took twenty-two engines, nine ladders, four rescue companies, a squad, three battalion chiefs, and two division chiefs to assist with the fire and recovery.

The whole operation lasted sixteen hours, and in the end, tragically, six firemen lost their lives and thirty-one were injured. The first deputy's job at this fire was to contact the chaplain and notify the family when there was a loss of life, and he made it his business to see that the injured were immediately provided with the proper medical treatment. Then the commissioner and Tom set up a makeshift command center in a nearby firehouse and kept the families informed on the status of their loved ones and where they were and how they could get in touch with them. It was the third worst disaster in the NYFD, until the events on September 11, 2001.

The first deputy commissioner was a gentle man with a caring and big heart. Tom recalls one morning when he thought he was picking up the commissioner to attend one of the funerals of three firemen who recently died in a fire at the Jolly Giant Restaurant on Liberty Avenue in Queens. When the deputy commissioner got in the car, Tom asked which funeral they would be attending first. The deputy said they would not be going to any of them. There would be plenty of firemen at each of those funerals; instead, they attended the funeral for a fireman who had been laid off from the job when the department was forced to make some cutbacks in order to save the City some money. Since he was one of the last group of firemen hired, he was among the first ones to be laid off. He was devastated and worked odd jobs while waiting patiently for the day he would be rehired, but he died suddenly. Strangely enough, the autopsy never revealed anything medically wrong. He was a fourth-generation fireman with a young family, and the layoff was particularly traumatic for him. His family was convinced that he died of a broken heart due to the years of waiting to finally fulfill his dream, only to be laid off and forced to leave the fire department.

At the funeral, the deputy told the widow that he would help her and her young child any way he could, and he kept that promise.

CHAPTER 26

Cooney would make trips back to his old firehouse in Harlem to talk with his buddies when he had some extra time between driving Mr. Buckley or the first deputy. At the end of one of those visits, the captain of the engine company took him aside and asked to talk with him. "Since you and Gerry left here, I have lost a few other good firemen from the house due to transfers," said the captain. The truck captain was also having the same problem. Tom told the captain he believed that the firemen in question had been in the Harlem firehouse for a long time, and if they wanted to go to a less busy house, they deserved the break. Tom noted that maybe for the sake of their families, they needed a place that put a little less strain on their bodies for the remainder of their careers. The captain reluctantly agreed but had to admit he personally hated losing

Tom, Gerry, and the others, saying the house just didn't seem the same without them.

Not long after the conversation with the captain, Cooney remembers coming home and finding his neighbor, also a NYC fireman, sitting in his kitchen visibly upset. The fireman worked in a firehouse about ten blocks from his old Harlem location and was upset because his car had been broken into and the car radio stolen. He said this was the second time the car had been damaged. A few months earlier, when he left the firehouse to go home after a night tour, he found his fender dented. During his time as a fireman, he worked in Brooklyn, the South Bronx, and then Harlem—all busy houses. He asked Tom if he might take his transfer request to his boss and see about getting into a firehouse in Staten Island. Cooney told him that getting a transfer to Staten Island would be "most improbable" or "nearly impossible," but he would give it a try. It took quite a few months, but eventually his friend's name appeared on the transfer list to a Staten Island firehouse, where he remained until his retirement. It was not that long ago that Tom was the one who needed help like this, and now he was the one being able to provide that same help to others. There were times when some unseen maneuvering behind the scenes played a part, and Tom conceded it helped "to know someone." For the time being, he was one of those someones.

Sometime in the early 1960s the fire department implemented a new system into their duty roster. It was designed to provide firemen some recovery time if their unit surpassed a certain number of runs and/or active fire duty on their first night shift. The plan was to then send that unit to recover at another, less busy firehouse on the second night shift.

One morning as Cooney reported to the Queens firehouse to pick up the first deputy's car, he noticed a different ladder truck parked out front. They were preparing to return to their busy firehouse in Brooklyn after switching for the night shift with a unit in Queens. Cooney joined the visiting firemen in the kitchen to chat and heard one of their young firemen remark that "Queens firemen have it made." He implied their job was easier because they had fewer runs and fires in their district. He had made several more comments along the same line when Cooney decided it was time to set the young fireman straight. He explained that most of the firemen in a Queens firehouse had worked for many years in some of the busiest firehouses in the City and had more than "paid their dues" before transferring to a firehouse in Queens. Cooney told him since he had only been on the job a few years, he still had much to learn, not only about the job, but about his fellow firefighters. He suggested it might be in his best interest to keep his comments to himself, until he had a chance to learn a little more about the job and get his facts straight.

Not to be outdone, the young fireman responded sarcastically, "Oh really, and where did you work before you became a driver for the first deputy?" Cooney told him he spent the better part of his career in a hook-and-ladder company at the firehouse on Lenox Avenue in Harlem. With that being said, a few of the firemen in the kitchen smiled at Tom and nodded in approval, while the others patted him on the shoulder as they were leaving. The young fireman was left standing there with nothing more to say.

CHAPTER 27

If being busy makes time go by faster, then it was certainly true for Cooney. Before he knew it, a few more years had gone by, and suddenly it was spring of 1978. But as it turned out, it was not going to be one of his better years.

"One day during my week of driving the first deputy, my partner, Gerry, stopped by the office and surprised me with the news that since he had recently accrued his twenty years with the fire department, he had put in his papers for retirement. He went on to say, he would now be able to devote himself to driving Mr. Buckley full time and would no longer need me as a partner. The unexpected words left me stunned, especially since he never even brought up the subject of retirement. Not to mention, I had grown quite fond of Mr. and Mrs. Buckley and my car companion, Rollie, and the thought of not seeing them again was upsetting. This all came as a complete surprise to me," Tom recalls, "and the additional loss of that much needed second income made it all very difficult to deal with." Mr. Buckley was also upset about the new arrangement and losing Tom. He wrote a strong letter of recommendation, which read in part, "Over a period of thirty years, I have not known a more dedicated, reliable, and cheerful man in any circumstance."

Mrs. Buckley, also concerned for Tom, was determined to find him another driving position, and sure enough she did. She heard from her close friend that her husband, a renowned plastic surgeon, was in need of a driver, and immediately contacted him to set up an appointment. When Tom arrived for the interview, the doctor was smiling. He began by saying that his wife had already called and said to do whatever he needed to do, "but please make sure you hire him," and he did. After the interview was over, Tom called Mrs. Buckley and thanked her for her kind gesture and recommendation and said he would begin his new job with the doctor in a few weeks. But as luck would have it, that job was never meant to be.

A week later, Cooney went to the firehouse to pick up the deputy's car at the firehouse, and the house watchman told him the commissioner needed the car as soon as possible. As one of the firemen jumped into the ladder truck to move it out of the way, Tom quickly picked up the heavy wooden chock from behind the truck so he could drive the car out—only to have it slip out of his hands and onto his left foot. He let out a moan and felt a sharp, searing pain. He ignored it as best he could and rushed to pick up the first deputy.

The deputy had just given Tom the destination address when the car radio informed them that the emergency had been averted and the first deputy was not needed after all. Instead they continued on to the office. When they got there, his boss noticed that Tom was limping and having difficulty walking. Tom told him what happened, and the deputy insisted he go to the medical office and have the foot examined. Preliminary x-rays showed multiple fractures, and the next day Tom went to see an orthopedist. Tom was put in a full-leg cast, confined to a wheelchair, and put on medical leave for six weeks. To make matters worse, he received a call from his new part-time employer, the plastic surgeon, who said he was sorry to hear about Tom's accident and was looking forward to working with him, but unfortunately he would be unable to hold the job open until he was well enough to drive again.

But the bad luck did not stop there. Even after Cooney got his cast off, he was still experiencing a great deal of pain when he walked and went back and forth between doctors for the next six months. After another six months of various treatments and physical therapy, the x-rays showed his foot had sustained permanent damage. A fire department doctor concluded that due to his limited weight-lifting and weight-bearing abilities, his days as an active firefighter should be over. Meanwhile, Tom continued his job as driver to the first deputy. Now, due to the constant foot pain, he was unable to work a second job, so his wife, comfortable with the fact that the children would be in school all day, found herself a secretarial position with a local surveying and engineering firm in town.

Things were just beginning to return to normal when the first deputy called Tom into his office for a chat. There was going to be a change of administration in City Hall soon, and his boss was not sure how much longer he would remain as first deputy. That meant Tom's job was also once again in jeopardy. He knew if his boss was let go, normally he would have been returned to his truck job at one of the firehouses, but that was no longer an option since he was declared medically unfit to resume fire duty. He thought maybe the fire department might try to find him some kind of a desk job at headquarters, but he was sure he would not be happy with that. So, after much deliberation, Tom decided that after twenty years on the job, maybe this was a sign. It was time for him to put in his papers for retirement.

Cooney left the New York Fire Department for good on Thursday, December 13, 1979. Tom said, "What made it easier for me to put my papers in for retirement was the fact that I had already been out of the Harlem firehouse for four years, and many of the firemen with whom I worked were now either working in other firehouses or retired.

"My last day on the job at fire headquarters was uneventful. I remember driving home from the City that last night and thinking about my twenty years on the job. I remembered the ceremony when I received my Badge #711 and how many times I like to think that number brought me luck and saved my hide (or kept me from serious harm). I thought about the many friends I made on the job who I am still friends with today. And I sadly remembered the many fire friends I lost and still grieve for. I remembered the many fireman parties, picnics, St. Patrick Day parades, and miscellaneous celebrations of the earlier years, and wondered how those years could have passed so quickly. They were good years and I consider myself a lucky man to have had a job to go to that I enjoyed for twenty years. The job never made me rich, but it gave me a sense of fulfillment that I was trained and able to help others in distress and proud to be a part of that brotherhood of men who were always there for you whether they were on duty or not. When I pulled into my driveway, I was greeted by my family, who were all happy that now my crazy hours and night tours were over. It was good to be home. Then it suddenly hit me: I had a wife, three children, and a mortgage—and I was unemployed!"

CHAPTER 28

"Some time later," Cooney said, "I was driving around town when I had to pull over to let a fire engine pass on their way to a call and decided to follow them. The fire was in a two-story building and when I arrived there, the engine company had stretched their hose into one of the first-floor fire rooms. I noticed no ladder company had responded, so I went over to the fire engine driver, told him I was a retired NYC fireman, and asked to borrow a six-foot hook. The driver gave me the hook, and I followed the hose line into fire room and started to pull the ceilings. The smoke was quite heavy for the men, even with the mask, so I suggested something to the nozzle man that I learned as a fireman. I suggested he open the nozzle to the spray position and aim it toward the window to help alleviate the smoke. He tried it and the smoke lifted, leaving the fireman to put out the fire with less difficulty."

When the fire was out, Cooney said the fireman looked at him in disbelief, standing there with no fire clothing on and wondering who he was and where he came from. Tom returned the hook to the fireman, said, "Thank you," and continued on his way home, leaving the firemen shaking their heads. When he arrived home all wet, his wife recognized that all-too-familiar smoke smell and was reluctant to ask him what happened. He told her how he had gotten sidetracked by the fire sirens on the way home and how he stopped and helped the local firemen. Tom said, "When I saw that fire engine responding on my way home, I suddenly felt the loss of not being a fireman anymore. Even the smoke smelled good to me. I guess there is some truth to the old adage, once a fireman, always a fireman."

Cooney did not stay retired for long. The next couple of months began a series of "retirement celebrations" from a variety of jobs. The first one after retiring was a job offer from the nephew of a friend who needed someone to act as crew supervisor during the installation of a new phone system for New York Hospital. Tom told the nephew his knowledge of telephone installation was very limited and was assured he would receive enough on-the-job training to manage the six-month job. However, the work crew proved to be fewer in number and more inexperienced than earlier promised, and the job went on for more than the original six months. The job also entailed constant climbing of stairs, which aggravated Tom's foot injury. So, after six months, he "retired."

Cooney then took a job as a chauffeur for a local limousine service. This job also turned out to be short lived. He was hired to be on call for eight hours at a time, but was never told that the hourly rate only applied to the actual hours he would be on the road with a client. In the early 1980s there was not much call for limousine service in his local area, so after two paychecks, Tom once again "retired."

His next step was to try something closer to home. He accepted a job in a local factory doing piecework. After only two weeks, he found himself watching the clock for the break call and listening for the lunch bell to break the monotony of just sitting still. He had too much energy stored up and needed to find something more suitable, so he "retired" again.

CHAPTER 29

After so many years of driving back and forth to work, driving for Mr. Buckley and then the first deputy commissioner, Cooney was really hoping to find a job closer to home. He was not happy with the few jobs he did try and was beginning to get discouraged when a friend called to let him know that the county jail was looking to hire additional corrections officers. Tom thought, *Why not give it a try?* and put in an application. It took less than two weeks for him to be called in for a interview. The interview with the warden lasted for about an hour, and when it was over, the warden decided to hire Tom immediately and asked him if he would be available to start the following week. He also said that because of the shortage of corrections officers, he would not be sent to the police academy, but rather receive on-the-job training. His wife teased him about being partial to blue uniforms and sent him off to his new job.

Sussex County Jail was a new, modern building that had large windows with no bars but were equipped with alarm sensors. In the event an inmate should bang on the window, it would trigger an alarm at the officer's command center. But the sensors did not always work properly and would go off and on intermittently, so the officers never knew for sure whether they were working or not. It did not take long for the inmates to catch on to this fact.

One evening when Cooney was working the four-to-twelve shift, his supervisor informed him that his shift partner had called in sick and he would be working his command center alone. During the inmates' nightly cleanup routine, there was always a lot of noise going on. They knew Tom was new on the job and alone in the command center and he would not be able to watch all the cells at once. So they took a chance and banged against the window. No alarm went off. Then they broke off a piece of metal from a desk and used it to pry open the window, tied a sheet to the bed, hung it out of the window, and escaped. Later when the duty officer came upstairs to take a bed count, he found five inmates missing. A search was conducted throughout the building and surrounding outside area, but none of the missing inmates were found. When relieved of his shift at midnight by the twelve-to-eight officer, Tom immediately went to see the warden. He said since it happened on his watch, he was sorry and would turn in his badge and uniform. Before he could say any more, the warden stopped him and said, "The breakout was not your fault; actually it was my fault, and I'll make sure this never happens again." Tom remained on the job, and the five inmates were all caught within a few months and returned to jail.

Cooney had been working at the county jail for about a year when he began working with a part-time corrections officer who happened to also be a state corrections officer. He mentioned to Tom several times that the test for the state prison system was coming up soon and he should give it some consideration. Tom started to give the idea some serious thought. He figured he was already working shifts, he would basically be doing the same job, and the annual salary was better, so why not give it a try? He took the next available test, received a high score, and within a year began his new job as a state corrections officer.

It was now 1983 and Tom was forty-nine years old. As a newly assigned officer at Annandale Prison, he was given a guided tour throughout the buildings. As he went from area to area, he heard his new fellow officers remark, in voices loud enough for him to hear, that he must not be thinking straight to become a corrections officer at such a relatively late age. He remained at the Annandale location for about a year and a half.

A downside of his new state job location was that

once again Tom found himself driving long distances to and from his place of employment. So when the opportunity presented itself, Tom put in a bid for a transfer. He applied for one of the openings at the state satellite facility located at Stokes State Forest, which was closer to his home. This particular facility held ninety inmates who had committed lesser crimes and had shorter sentences to serve. They were not confined in individual jail cells; rather they were housed in rooms more along the lines of army barracks, but with no bars on the windows. As a condition of their sentence at this facility, each day they would be assigned into groups, under the supervision of an officer, and bussed to an area for community service. They would then spend the day either picking up trash along the state highway, cutting grass in the state park, or cleaning up the state campsites. As was to be expected, a certain amount of complaining took place among the inmates from time to time about the park duty, especially from the city boys.

Cooney also recalls that the satellite unit did not have a doctor at the facility, so if an inmate became ill he would have to be driven to a prison medical center. The closest one to the facility was in the maximum security prison building in Trenton. As it happened, one of the constant complainers hurt himself in the park and needed to be taken to the medical facility in Trenton. When they arrived, the inmate watched in disbelief as the corrections officer was patted down and then he was patted down and strip-searched. Security officers were everywhere, and he was startled when, during examination and treatment, he was handcuffed to the bed. When he returned to the Stokes facility, Tom asked him how it went, and he quickly replied, "I never want to be in that jail or even go back to that place again." None of the officers ever heard him complain about park duty again.

Cooney was not working at the Stokes Forest facility very long when it came to the attention of his supervisors that he was a retired New York City fireman and they inquired if he would be willing to put some of his background knowledge to good use. He asked what they had in mind, and a month later he was appointed fire marshal of the facility. Tom set up fire prevention classes and programs that would instruct the staff how to handle and use the fire extinguishers. He also taught the officers how to properly wear and use the Scott Air Packs in the event of an emergency. In addition to his fire prevention programs, he also arranged to have the local fire department visit the facility to conduct a fire drill with the inmates.

Cooney had been working as a state corrections officer for almost two years when someone in the main office noticed he had never been sent to complete his corrections officers' training academy requirement in Trenton. So, at fifty-one years of age, Tom found himself back in a barracks just like during his military days, sleeping on double bunk beds and being awoken at 5 a.m. to do physical exercises and run around the track. There was a group of young body-builders in his unit who he suspected would intentionally mess up on their pushup count so the instructors would make everyone start again, just to see if "the old man" could keep up. But somehow Tom made it through and was able to complete the needed course and fulfill his missing requirement.

After a few years working at this facility, Cooney was able to obtain an assignment as one of the supervising officers who would accompany a group of inmates to work duty in the parks. He was happy to receive this assignment because it now meant now he would only be working day shifts. One day when Cooney took the inmates out for the daily park work program, he noticed one of the new inmates continually staring at him while raking leaves. Finally, after a few minutes, Tom went over to him and asked the inmate if he was having a problem. The inmate said no, but he thought Tom looked familiar. Tom replied that it was probably from one of the other jails. The inmate didn't think so and left it at that. A few days later, the same inmate approached Tom again and said he remembered from where he knew him. He said, "You were the fireman that drove the tiller on the ladder truck in my Harlem neighborhood and gave out cookies at Christmas." Tom smiled when he heard that. He did not remember the boy, but he did remember the firehouse and certainly the neighborhood he came from. When the young inmate finished his time and was leaving to go home, Tom told him he did not want to see him back at the facility again and made him promise he would stay out of trouble. The young man said he had learned his lesson and he would let Tom know how he was doing. Tom had a very positive feeling about him and was sure he would not see him back in prison again. He was happy to note that the last he heard from him, he had a steady job, had gotten married, and was looking to start a family.

Cooney continued to work as a state corrections officer for the next eleven years before he started having thoughts of "retirement" again. He had only been retired for six short months, and while he enjoyed not having to get up early anymore, he found himself getting a little bored at times. So, when he saw an ad calling for a part-time driver at an alcohol and drug rehabilitation facility, he filled out an application and got the job. Part of his job description was to pick up clients at their homes and bring them to the facility to complete a thirty-day rehabilitation treatment program. The residents were from all parts of New Jersey and New York and sometimes spent hours in the car with Tom, riding up to the facility. Some of the men and women he brought to the center were private clients who entered on their own, while others were required to seek treatment by their employer or by order of the court. Many clients, knowing full well they would not be allowed to drink anything but juice for the next thirty days, would have a last drink and be in an exceptionally happy mood when he arrived. Others would be quite apprehensive and during the ride try to convince Tom to turn around and bring them back home. To help calm the client, Tom would sometimes pull off to the side of the road and talk with them and answer any questions they might have about the facility. At the end of the conversation, the nervous client would usually relent and agree to try the program. In the eighteen months he worked at this job, Tom is pleased to say he never had a client refuse to complete the trip.

In March of 1997, Tom and Edie became the proud grandparents with the birth of their grandson, Corey James, who was on born St. Patrick's Day morning. Three months later, their daughter found it necessary to return to work, so Tom volunteered to become the designated babysitter. When the hours of his part-time driving job began to conflict with his daily babysitting duties, he retired one more time. The bond between Pop-Pop and grandson was instant, and Tom was never bored again.

Years later in February 2000, their daughter made them proud grandparents again with the birth of Tyler Thomas. Mrs. Cooney decided that perhaps handling one toddler and one infant might be a bit much for Tom, so she also retired and joined her husband in their new babysitting adventure. Edie was delighted to be home and have an infant and toddler to fuss over once again. They fed, dressed, played, laughed, and took the boys on outings. Their days were active and it kept them young. It also gave them the chance to relive the many wonderful memories they shared of their early days as parents.

So by February 2000, Cooney had been retired for almost three years and was looking forward to enjoying his golden years with his wife of forty-six years. After working hard for so long, in many vital lines of work, Tom was now enjoying his retirement, being able to sit back, relax, and spend time with his grown children and grandchildren. Then came September 11, 2001.

CHAPTER 30

The morning of Tuesday, September 11, 2001, began as a bright, clear, late summer day. Cooney recalls being suddenly awakened by his wife, who told him that a plane had just crashed into one of the twin towers at the World Trade Center in Manhattan. Cooney remembers getting up to watch the newscast, and immediately a second plane struck the other tower. Cooney sat glued to the television set, watching in total disbelief as suddenly one tower collapsed. Within minutes, so did the second one. Knowing how many firemen must have been inside the buildings trying to help the people escape the chaos and seeing the fire trucks buried under piles of rubble, Tom and his wife stared in stunned silence and wept. Over 3,000 men and women lost their lives that day, and 343 of them were firemen.

Later in the day, a fireman friend called Tom to tell

him one of the missing firemen was their old buddy from the Harlem unit, Bill Feehan. Tom remembers Bill used to kid him about them starting out the same way—both growing up in New York City and going into the army right after high school and always wanting to be a fireman. After Bill's discharge from the army, he went on to earn a degree from St. John's University. While he could have had several other jobs, he wanted to be a fireman and in 1959 he got his wish. When the lieutenant's test came up, he took that and easily passed it and did the same with the promotion test for captain. Tom got to know him well when he was assigned to his firehouse in Harlem as captain of Engine Company 59, the same house as Ladder Company 30 and Squad Unit #1. At the time, headquarters felt the Harlem firehouse was a little too lax with the fire department rules and wanted Captain Feehan to try to "tighten up the house" a bit. After Captain Feehan had been at the house for a few months, headquarters called to see how things were going. The captain responded that after watching the three fire companies in action, he wasn't about to change a thing.

Bill continued to work his way up through the ranks of the fire department, and Tom would meet up with him from time to time during his years as driver for the first deputy. By the early 1990s he had achieved the rank of chief of the NYFD, the highest rank that can be attained. He held that position until he was forced to retire at the age of sixty-five. However, he was so highly regarded by the fire department that they asked him to become first deputy commissioner. And so it was that on September 11, 2001, Bill Feehan was at his command post in the towers when the first tower crumbled to the ground and buried him. He was barely alive when they rescued him and unfortunately succumbed to his injuries a few days later. After forty-one years on the job, he sadly became one of the 343 firemen who perished that day. His son is also a fireman and is following in his father's footsteps.

In the days that followed, Cooney was visibly upset and as he continued to watch the newscasts at home, he began thinking about the 23rd Street fire so many years before. He remembered how it had taken nearly a thousand firemen a full day to dig out the material from a five-story building in order to recover the twelve trapped firemen. Cooney realized that the fire department was going to need all the help it could get, so he decided to make the trip to the Manhattan site and offer his services. His wife was anxious about his decision, but knew he had to go. She just asked that he please be careful and try to remember that he was sixty-seven, not thirty-seven years old anymore. Tom promised to keep that in mind and drove down to his old firehouse in Harlem. He showed them his old #711 fire badge and said he was on his way down to Ground Zero. They told him to leave his car with them because there was no place to park where he was going. They then asked if he had any fire clothing with him, but after being retired for twenty-two years, all he had left was his helmet, and he was wearing work boots. They opened a locker and gave him a turnout coat that a fireman had left behind when he retired and found him a pair of work gloves. Before he left, they showed him how they had set up the back room of the firehouse as sleeping quarters where the firemen who were coming from all over the country could catch some shut-eye after working at Ground Zero. They wished him luck and Tom left to take the subway to his destination downtown.

During his ride, as people were getting on and off the train, they took notice of his fire gear and approached him to say thank you. Many of them simply wanted to shake his hand. He was particularly taken aback by the many who warned him to be careful, while others quietly said, "God bless you." By the time Tom reached his train stop, he was a little unnerved by the experience, since he knew New York City train riders generally kept to themselves and mostly liked to ride in silence. He soon came to understand the reason for their reactions.

CHAPTER 31

As Cooney climbed the exit stairs of the subway, the smell of the dense smoke rising from the towers filled his nostrils. He walked a few blocks closer to the site and came to a barricade, where a soldier asked him, "Fire department?" Cooney replied yes, and the barricade was opened for him to walk through. He smiled, remembering the words his former deputy commissioner had told him the night Tom attended the Heisman trophy dinner by mistake. "If you act like you belong, no one will question you." And that advice just rang true once again.

Cooney decided the best place to start was at the firehouse that faced the south tower. As he got nearer to the site, he was shaken by how much it had begun to resemble a war zone. The devastation was beyond comprehension. He was further startled by the sight of a huge piece of shining steel that stuck out like a spear in the remains of what was once an office building. Tom admits as he got closer to the site, his emotions got the best of him, especially as he looked around the surrounding area and saw the remains of the south tower. There stood a fire truck, with its aerial fully extended, next to a huge pile of debris, and even with the ladder raised to that height, it could not reach the top of the remains of bricks and steel from the collapsed tower.

Cooney found the chief at the site and asked where he could be of some help. The chief directed him toward the block where the fire companies were working and told him where to enter the tower plaza. Tom made his way to the area and was surprised to learn he had to climb down: The plaza floor had collapsed below the street. It was then that he began to realize the horror and enormity of what had happened. As Tom carefully began his descent to the collapsed floor level, he looked up and could see the other buildings with their outer walls completely gone, damaged cars still parked on the garage floor and on the floors above, and office desks and chairs twisted and scattered about. When he reached the floor level, he met a police officer who was working with his search dog. The officer told him the search was very frustrating because the poor dog would react each time he came to an opening in the collapsed floor, but there was nothing they were able to do except report it. They were still waiting for the arrival of the heavy cranes needed to lift up the huge sections of cement slabs. But, he continued, they would keep searching on the slim chance they might find someone still alive closer to the surface. The policeman and his dog were obviously exhausted, but refused to stop their search. It was sadly becoming all too obvious to Tom that this would be more of a recovery operation than the rescue mission everyone was desperately hoping for.

Cooney continued on and located a fire chief and asked where he could be the most help. The chief sent him to help the fire companies that were presently running hose lines to put out the many fires still burning beneath floors of the tower plaza. Tom spent the next eight hours pulling hoses and pouring water onto these fires that could not be reached but continued to erupt, from place to place, beneath the floors of the tower plaza.

On his second time back at Ground Zero, before he made his descent down the long ramp to the work area, he decided to stop for a quick New York lunch, which consisted of a hot dog and soda, sold by a push-cart vendor. As he waited in line, the man in front of him started a conversation with Tom and asked why he bothered going down to work in the tower debris when clearly there was no one left alive. Tom responded by explaining that if he were to find only one item from a lost individual and if that item would help a grieving family member of that person find closure, then what he was doing would be well worth the time and effort. After listening to his explanation, the stranger then turned around and paid for Tom's lunch.

The tedious work of digging through the massive rubble at the site involved scraping up the material and putting it into dump trucks, which would then go a short distance to a cleared area, about the size of a football field, dump the material, and spread it out. Then the recovery workers would start at one end, sifting through the material with three-pronged rakes, and go through the entire pile. When they reached the other end, they would turn around and re-check the pile the same way, working their way back to where they began. If and when they found something that might be of possible emotional value, it would then be separated and placed in a special container, and the rest of the material would be put back on a truck and taken to specified dumping sites.

Cooney would return to Ground Zero as often as he could, sometimes taking a day or a week in between to rest his sore muscles. Each time he returned he was amazed by the number of other retired firemen and firefighters—from all over the country—who were also there, all working alongside the regular New York firemen on duty. Tom said, "There is no doubt in my mind that the cleanup of the towers could not have been completed within eight months' time without the help of all the volunteers who came to the site day after day. During my time in the fire department, I was involved in many rescue and recovery operations, but it was painful to see a retired fireman, about my age, digging next to me with a picture of his fireman son on the front piece of his helmet, looking to find his son. What can you say to him? Sights like this just broke my heart."

Cooney went down to Ground Zero several more times to work at the devastated site during the recovery process, which lasted for months. Each time he went, he would remain at the site for eight to ten hours, then take the subway to the firehouse to pick up his car and make the long ride back home.

"On one of the days when I was down working at the site, a fire lieutenant approached me and said he noticed my old company number on my helmet and wanted to know when I had worked there. We started a conversation and the lieutenant asked me why he had not seen me at the retired firemen luncheons that Ladder 30 and Engine 59 held a couple times a year. I told him I was unaware the luncheons were taking place or I would have been there. The lieutenant then took my name and address and said he would definitely put me on the mailing list. He was true to his word and I soon started getting notices and began attending the luncheons. I was delighted to be reunited with some of my old buddies and hash over stories with other retired firefighters."

CHAPTER 32

In the first week of April 2002, Cooney was back at the towers for the last time. He was digging on the side of a remaining pile of the north tower, while the heavy cranes were at work on the other side. It was close to evening break when one of the cranes pulled on a steel girder, which in turn moved the pile that a couple of men were standing on and knocked them and Cooney off their feet. Cooney went down on his left knee, and when he got up, he saw it was scraped and bruised, but not enough to require medical attention, or so he thought. The men stopped working and took their evening break, climbing up to street level and over to the tent, where they were provided with some hot food. By the time they were ready to return to work, Tom's knee was painfully throbbing, so he told the men he was working with that he was going home. After a few days the throbbing subsided, but he noticed the knee-cap had a small pea-sized lump on it. When the lump failed to go away, he went to see his doctor. An x-ray revealed nothing broken, and since he was having no acute pain, the doctor recommended some hot soaks and to keep an eye out for any changes.

Tom paid little attention to it until a few weeks later, when he was playing on the floor with his grandson, and he noticed it was painful to kneel on his left knee. When he checked, he was surprised to see that the lump had grown into a soft mass, about the size of a golf ball, and covered his kneecap. His doctor referred him to an orthopedic surgeon, who, in turn, scheduled Tom for surgery to remove what appeared to be a cyst. After the surgery, the doctor told him he had removed what he could, but it looked suspicious and he was sending a biopsy to the laboratory for testing. He then gave Mrs. Cooney the name of a highly recommended surgeon who specialized in musculoskeletal oncology at University Hospital in Newark. He told her to contact him immediately because he suspected the growth was not benign.

When the biopsy report came back from the lab, it indicated the mass was a fast-growing sarcoma, which would require additional surgery. A few weeks later, Tom underwent a seven-hour surgery to remove the sarcoma and to reconstruct his knee, which entailed using a calf muscle to fill in the empty space in the kneecap and a skin graft to cover the kneecap. Cooney spent a week in the hospital and then, as an outpatient, traveled back and forth to University Hospital daily for five weeks for radiation treatments.

Next, arrangements were made for Tom to have physical therapy at home, three times a week, to help him regain his mobility. To this day, Cooney still marvels at the skillful job the surgeon did on his leg and continues to credit his therapist for his being able to walk now as well as he did before the operation. Cooney remarked, "My two young grandsons would be here during the day and quietly watch as she put me through my paces. Each time she went to leave, they would run to give her a hug to thank her for helping Pop-Pop to walk again." Tom remembers that she made him work hard and there were times he wanted to quit, but she was determined to get him back up on both feet and walking so he could continue to play with his grandchildren. And he will always be grateful, because she made that happen.

In 2007, Cooney received an invitation to attend the 100th anniversary celebration of Ladder Company 30. When he arrived that morning, the firehouse was already packed with both past and present Ladder 30 and Engine 59 members, and Cooney recalls it felt great to see all his old buddies again and to talk over old times. Tom was looking around the firehouse and as he was entering the truck office, he bumped into someone with a lot of gold stripes on his sleeve, so he quickly apologized. "Why, Tom Cooney, don't you remember me?" the man asked. It was Tom Jenson, who was still on the job, but was now the chief in charge of fire prevention for the City of New York. The two had worked together for a time in 1973, when Jensen was first assigned to Ladder 30. Today he was at the anniversary celebration as one of several guest speakers during the plaque ceremony. As the current members of Ladder 30 stood at attention in full uniform on the apparatus floor, Cooney looked around and noted that "they all seemed so very young."

The doctors kept a close eye on Cooney after his knee surgery, with continuing follow-up visits and tests every six months. Things went well for a few years, until 2008, when Cooney's doctor noticed a black spot on his right earlobe during a routine examination. He sent him to a specialist for a biopsy, and the results were once again troublesome. The doctor reviewed the biopsy report, which indicated it was a stage three melanoma, and put Tom in touch with a wonderful oncologist surgeon to discuss the necessary surgery. The surgery was performed in two stages. First the melanoma and a lymph node behind his ear were removed, and two weeks later, an additional sixteen lymph nodes were removed from the side of his neck.

Now it was time for Tom to consult with a second oncologist, who would administer his forty-two weeks of chemotherapy treatments, three times a week, at a cancer center. After five months, Tom was so sick from the treatments that he could not keep any food down, lost forty pounds, became disoriented, had trouble walking, and always needed to sleep. The doctors took notice and decided to halt the treatments, since they felt that he had already gotten the most benefit from them and the rest were precautionary. Within a few weeks after stopping, Tom was able to slowly eat again, began to regain his strength, and started to feel much better. However, Tom's oncologist is taking no chances with her patient. She makes sure he is at her office every three to six months for blood work and x-rays and that he sees his dermatologist in between visits.

Ten years after 9/11, the federal government recognized a direct link of certain types of cancer, including melanoma and sarcoma, to those involved in the events of 9/11. But Cooney steadfastly refuses to file any claim, despite his having suffered from these diseases. "I'm not looking for a reward for what I did," he said.

In 2009, Cooney was in his local library checking out books, and he noticed a sign asking anyone with items of interest to the public to contact the librarian. Cooney went home and took out his fire department material; he decided that he would put together a special memorial display in order to honor the 343 firemen who were killed on 9/11. This display included photos of all the lost firemen and some small items Cooney got at Ground Zero, such as a piece of glass from one of the fallen tower windows, a piece of plastic from the grille of a buried fire truck, and a clip that had held the hose on the standpipe of the towers, also two steel bolts. The display was at the library for an entire month and was warmly received. A friend of Cooney's, a retired teacher, saw the display and called him to suggest that local schools might be interested in having him show his display.

The local schools were more than interested, and soon Tom was bringing his display to schools all over New Jersey and lower New York State. He also received requests to set up the display at public libraries and in bank lobbies.

By September 2010, the commemorative material garnered some attention in the press, and it ended up on the Internet. One night just before midnight, Cooney received a phone call from a sixth grade student who lived in California and had obviously forgotten about the time difference on the East Coast. He said he called to ask Tom if he would be willing to answer a few questions about 9/11 and his display. At first Tom thought it was a prank, but the young boy said he had read about the display in a newspaper article written about him on the Internet and decided to do a school report about it. Convinced that the young boy was serious, Tom spoke with him for a while and happily answered all his questions. A few weeks later he received a note from the sixth grader, thanking him for taking the time, He told Tom he got a good grade on his report. Included in the envelope was also a note of appreciation from the young boy's teacher.

Cooney is deeply proud of and emotionally drawn to what the commemorative display represents, and is more than happy and willing to display it anywhere there may be interest. "They may be gone, but they won't be forgotten," Cooney said of the fallen firemen.

EPILOGUE

Tom, today at eighty years young, despite the injuries and illness he sustained over the years, is still spry and seems in far better shape than many men his age. He and his wife, Edie, now married for nearly six decades, spend most of their free time enjoying the company of their family, friends, and especially their grandchildren. Two of the grandchildren are very active in basketball and baseball, and Tom gets great pleasure from attending their many games. Even though his children have long-since grown and do not all live in the area, he keeps in close touch with them.

Cooney has never backed away from a day of work and still maintains his own lawn and garden in summer, shovels as needed in winter, and continues to be actively involved with his 911 Memorial Display.

So far as Tom knows, he is free of the knee sarcoma

that once caused such havoc in his life. As for the melanoma, it is currently in remission and remains an "unknown quantity," so he must continue his scheduled oncologist visits for constant checkups.

With good health continuing, he is looking forward to celebrating his 80th birthday and his 60th wedding anniversary in 2014. "Edie and I have always been a team," states Cooney. "We were young and in love and began our marriage with $100 between us. We had a rough start with some hard times, but we were happy, worked hard, and it all came together. I was a New York City fireman and loved my job; I have a wife and three great children and some grandchildren, and here we are in our golden years. What more could I ask for?"

One of the outings that Cooney still looks forward to is attending the luncheons that take place a couple times each year with his former fire department comrades. However, thirty-five years have passed since his days on the job, and some of the faces he sees there are unfamiliar to him. Tom said, "It makes me realize how quickly time has passed. More than half of the men now present at the luncheons came to my old firehouse after I left, and some have even since retired. I may be considered an old-timer by these younger retirees, but I still enjoy meeting with them and listening to their stories, while sharing some of mine with them."

Today Tom and Edie continue to live in the same house that started as a "shell" and grew into a home fifty years ago. Tom is a quiet, kind, and loyal friend who takes great pride in his past. Tom is also a sensitive man who, with a heavy heart, still remembers all his fellow firefighters who were seriously injured or who lost their lives, doing the job they chose and were trained to do. Yet if you ask him, he will tell you, if given the chance, he would do it all over again.

Cooney counts his blessings, knowing full well what a fortunate man he really is. He will always have two families; one being his loved ones and the other his brotherhood of former firefighters. He is also grateful, as we all should be, there will always be men and women who are willing to dedicate their lives and take chances for the safety and welfare of others. They deserve our gratitude whether they are city-paid professionals or local town volunteers. They are always there, prepared and ready to respond to your call.

CPSIA information can be obtained at www.ICGtesting.com
Printed in the USA
BVOW08s2205200714

359795BV00006B/32/P